Divine Secrets

OF

MENTORING

SPIRITUAL GROWTH THROUGH FRIENDSHIP

CAROL BRAZO

InterVarsity Press
Downers Grove, Illinois

InterVarsity Press
P.O. Box 1400, Downers Grove, IL 60515-1426
World Wide Web: www.ivpress.com
E-mail: mail@ivpress.com

InterVarsity Press® is the book-publishing division of InterVarsity Christian Fellowship/USA®, a student movement active on campus at hundreds of universities, colleges and schools of nursing in the United States of America, and a member movement of the International Fellowship of Evangelical Students. For information about local and regional activities, write Public Relations Dept., InterVarsity Christian Fellowship/USA, 6400 Schroeder Rd., P.O. Box 7895, Madison, WI 53707-7895, or visit the IVCF website at <www.ivcf.org>.

All Scripture quotations, unless otherwise indicated, are taken from the Holy Bible, New International Version®. NIV®. Copyright ©1973, 1978, 1984 by International Bible Society. Used by permission of Zondervan Publishing House. All rights reserved.

Design: Cindy Kiple

Images: Ann Suma/Getty Images

ISBN 0-8308-3237-8

Printed in the United States of America ∞

Library of Congress Cataloging-in-Publication Data

Brazo, Carol Jo.
  Divine secrets of mentoring: spiritual growth through friendship/
  Carol Brazo.
    p. 3m.
  ISBN 0-8308-3237-8 (pbk.: alk. paper)
  1. Christian women—Religious life. 2. Mentoring in church work.
  I. Title.
  BV4527B684 2004
  248.8'43—dc22
                                                                  2004004354

| P | 18 | 17 | 16 | 15 | 14 | 13 | 12 | 11 | 10 | 9 | 8 | 7 | 6 | 5 | 4 | 3 | 2 |
| Y | 18 | 17 | 16 | 15 | 14 | 13 | 12 | 11 | 10 | 09 | 08 | 07 | 06 | 05 | 04 |

. . . .

For Cathy Gray,
sister to my soul.

. . . .

Contents

· ·

Acknowledgments

. . . .

No book is written in isolation. This book belongs to the women whose stories teach through its pages. I am forever grateful to those of you who have so graciously shared your journey with me. You are sisters to my soul.

I am deeply indebted to Cindy Bunch and Penny Kirk for their editing work. These women took a batch of dearly loved stories and formed them into a book. I cannot thank you enough for your guidance and your patience. Janet Kobobel-Grant is the definition of a fine agent. Your faith in my work has been more sustaining than you will ever know.

I would also like to thank the Hemstreet Foundation of St. Barnabas Church, McMinnville, Oregon. Your fund to support the spiritual growth of women is incredible. Thank you for encouraging my own learning curve.

The George Fox University family is amazing. Thank you for your patience and support as I juggled family, school, work and writing. I have the best job on the planet.

Finally, I am blessed by my own family. Mark, you are my heart. Your care and persistence are the reason anything gets written. Megan, Rachael and Noah, you are the joy of my heart. I love you more than you will ever know. And Dad, you are the rock. There are no words to tell you what your faithful life means to me.

Introduction

. . . .

M*entor*. I just do not like the word. I can be a friend or a teacher, but don't call me mentor. So, naturally, that is what my young friend did.

We were having lunch at a new little French café in town. Anne and her husband had recently put a down payment on a home being built just blocks from mine. She had asked me to lunch, and I was excited to hear about her plans to move to our town. I was anxious to talk house and decorating and gardening. I wanted to do the girl-friend bit, but then she went and ruined it all with the *M* word.

"So," she began, "you're my mentor and I wanted to . . ." She stopped abruptly, having read my face correctly. I was aghast.

"Uh, should I have asked?" she said, laughing. I stumbled around a bit and finally confessed that I wasn't very sure of that word, *mentor*. It is a business word to me, and while Anne is a rising star at Nike, I have absolutely no business sense at all. It is a career word, not a friend word. I wanted to be Anne's friend.

This was the start of an interesting study in words for me. *Mentor*, as Anne quickly explained, means coach, adviser, guide, instructor. (The thesaurus also lists words like *teacher, trainer* and *partner*.) These were friendlier words. Words I could eat lunch to. Words that implied a walking-side-by-side kind of relationship.

We laughed through lunch. Anne had a list of questions to ask me that led us down some interesting paths. I like Anne. I like her questions. She makes me think deeply about life and she challenges some of my assumptions. I was sad when the lunch hour ended and we had to head off to work.

I walked to my car, musing about mentors and mentoring. As I thought about it, I realized I had been blessed with a life full of wonderful mentors. Now the tables were turned: I was being asked to mentor. I didn't like the pressure I was beginning to feel—pressure to be perfect, to know all the answers.

The Holy Spirit is wonderful. By the time I'd hit the first stoplight, I was reminded of Ernestine and the look on her face the first time I introduced her to a friend as "my mentor." She raised her eyebrow, shook her head and sighed. "I'm Ernestine," she told my friend. "I'm not her mentor."

I remembered my confusion. I was hurt at first, thinking that she didn't want to claim me as a student, that she didn't want me to be her "mentoree." I was uncomfortable, thinking that I had been presumptuous to name myself as her student. I decided to just let it go and hope she would continue to see me.

She did. She does. Ernestine *sees* me, in all the wonder of that word. She sees me more clearly than I often see myself. She has now been my mentor and friend for twenty-some years, and she knows me well. She knows the impulsive, rash parts of my character. She knows my weaknesses. She also knows my passion for Jesus, my love for Mark and the kids. She knows the scars that mark the most difficult bends in my road and is aware of their tenderness and need for care.

Ernestine is not my only mentor. I have been blessed with a circle of women who have taught me and coached me, been my cheerleaders and heard my heartbroken confessions.

My cooking is almost up to snuff, thanks to their continual help.

Their walks have also schooled me. Their willingness to share both victories and painful lessons from their own journeys with the Savior has instructed me.

So how do these relationships begin? What does it take to find an Ernestine? What do mentors teach and what do we do when someone seems to be learning from us? How do we find sisters who will be with us for the whole journey or for a special chapter in our lives? What do mentors teach us and when do we, in turn, become mentors?

Snuggle up under your favorite quilt, grab a cup of coffee, and let's examine together the dance of mentoring.

How Do I Find a Mentor?

. . . .

But Ruth replied, "Don't urge me to leave you or to turn back from you. Where you go I will go, and where you stay I will stay. Your people will be my people and your God my God. Where you die I will die, and there I will be buried. May the Lord deal with me, be it ever so severely, if anything but death separates you and me."

RUTH 1:16-17

RUTH'S STORY

They just didn't get it, couldn't understand. My family thought I was nuts to leave home and follow a sad-faced little woman to another country. They thought I had lost my senses.

And some of what they said was right. Naomi was grief stricken. She didn't even want my company. She begged Orpah and me to return home, to give her peace in her sorrow and allow her to travel alone. Orpah did return, but I just couldn't leave that little woman.

I'm not at all like Orpah. You see, I tend to be a bit stubborn, and I was determined to see Naomi laugh again. I had lived with her when she was whole, worshiping her strange God, full of laughter and dance. I loved this joy-filled woman, who danced as she sang of the miracles of Yahweh. I loved the sound of her laughter and the spontaneous hugs she gave me, hugs I had hungered for since I was a child. She was giving me something I had never had before. She was showing me how to play, how to laugh and enjoy life.

So I set my face, smiled at my family and at Naomi, and refused to leave her. I would not leave this woman until I had learned to laugh, and to laugh for a lifetime. I wanted to learn how to hug and to hold on to the good in life. I needed a teacher, and Naomi was the only woman I knew who could do it.

I know this sounds odd. I know that many who read our story don't understand why I had to follow her. Engulfed by grief, Naomi was instructing everyone within earshot to call her bitter. She wanted to be named by the tragedy she had suffered. But I knew better. I had seen Naomi whole. I wanted that same wholeness for myself. And if wholeness meant following the one God, the one who made Naomi smile in spite of herself, lifting her arms to encompass his creation, then I needed Naomi. I needed her to introduce me to the ways of this God and to the joy found there.

Besides, grief passes. I know it sounds harsh, but time eventually heals you to the place that the grief no longer flattens you. Naomi would eventually be able to experience worship without sobs. The day would come when she would fall asleep with dry eyes. I might even hear her laughter again. I was determined to hear her laughter again.

So I followed her home. I went looking for her laughter. I did as she told me, never understanding but following anyway. I worked as she worked. I slept by a handsome man's feet and found kindness there. Eventually I placed our child in her arms and felt Naomi's laughter as it reverberated off my bones and into my heart.

Most important, I learned to follow Naomi's heart. I learned to listen, as she did, to the words of Yahweh. I learned to obey his commands and to walk as his children walked. I learned to lift my own arms, to look at his creation with awe and wonder. I learned to laugh and to love and to hug my own children whenever the mood struck.

My children grew up safe and secure. No child sacrifice for my children. My children worship a God of love and of joy. We worship Naomi's God.

. . . .

THE NEED FOR MENTORS

Ruth followed Naomi for reasons of love. She needed the love, friendship and guidance of another woman, of an older, more experienced woman. Her story is filled with the kind of love and commitment that we hunger for as women.

There are myriad ways in which we are mentored and in which we mentor. Mentoring is a kaleidoscope, a constantly changing field of color and wonder. It is not a linear path on which one chooses *one* guide and faithfully imitates. Mentoring and being mentored are full of faces and circumstances and discovery. Mentoring is a rich tapestry woven by a community of generous souls.

I grew up surrounded by a community of women who loved God. I had a mom who worshiped Jesus, grandmothers who taught my parents to worship Jesus and aunties who worshiped Jesus—and still do.

My mother's circle of friends was packed with women who loved Jesus. I grew up with Annis teaching me Scripture, Ginger directing my social life back to the boundaries provided by Scripture, Virginia and Mary Etta providing comfort and wonderful food at every turn, and Fenter singing God's praises.

It was an incredible community in which to come of age. These women taught me most of what I know about the joys of being created in God's image. This is not to say that the men in my life had no influence. My dad and grandpas and uncles all added treasure to my life. They taught me the joy and fun of being a cherished daughter in a community of men who love and serve Jesus. But it was the women in my life who modeled and affirmed all I know about what it means to be female, created in God's image.

In Scripture, Titus 2:3-5 instructs:

> Likewise, teach the older women to be reverent in the way they live, not to be slanderers or addicted to much wine, but to teach what is good. Then they can train the younger women to love their husbands and children, to be self-controlled and pure, to be busy at home, to be kind, and to be subject to their husbands, so that no one will malign the word of God.

Scripture sets up a tall order. I have been blessed in life to have a circle of mentors, a wide circle of women who have loved me, taught me, laughed with me and sobbed with me. None of them would say they "mentored" me. They are probably uncomfortable with the word, even though they practice the concept on a regular basis. Yet most of us understand Ruth's need for Naomi. We see women whose lives hold elements we desire, things we have no idea how to possess. We hunger for a mentoring relationship.

FIRST MENTOR

My mother was my first and most profound mentor. She is the mentor whose words are stored in my bones, coming back to me on a daily basis, instructing me in how to live and how to love. Mom has been at Jesus' house now for six years, and not a day passes when I do not miss her, missing her special brand of wisdom.

I was in my twenties before I realized that not everyone had the good fortune to have a mom like mine. Mom and I were best friends as adults. She was the first call I made whenever I was stuck in a decision-making process. She was my closest female friend.

Mom taught me how to love. Even as I write these words, I can hear her arguing with my conclusion. She was so aware of her short-comings, so aware of her own sins, that she failed to take inventory of her strengths. But the reality is, she taught me how to love.

My mother loved my father with an intensity that grounded me as a child. I always knew that Mom's first love was Dad. He was the star around which she orbited. They held hands, always. She spoke well of him, always. She wanted to share her thoughts and experiences with him, always.

I remember when I was just weeks away from my wedding. Mom and I were in the car, on our way to order flowers. And because my mom had only ever spoken well of my father, she suddenly had a concern.

"Honey, you, uh . . . Carol, you know your Dad is not perfect, right?" she asked, while negotiating the freeway.

I glanced at her and laughed. "Right, Saint William is not perfect." I adore my father. He walks with Jesus. But I had been a normal teenager. I had rows with both parents that make me cringe today. At twenty-five, memories of those conflicts were fresh. I knew Dad was not perfect. I had helped him understand that on numerous occasions!

"Seriously, Carol," Mom cautioned.

"Seriously, Mom," I sighed.

We drove another mile or two before she picked up the thread again. "Carol, you know your dad and I have had disagreements in our marriage," she said, eyes on the road.

I glanced at her, wondering what this was all about. In my childhood, I had only seen my parents have a serious disagreement once. It had been resolved by their quick trip to the beach while my sister and I were farmed out to Grandma. I had seen little of the flare-up and none of the resolution.

"Ongoing disagreements?" I asked.

Mom's smile was an easy one. "Ongoing as in rehashing the same mistakes? Then yes. Ongoing as in, are we fighting and in trouble? No." She sounded amused.

"So what is the point of all this?" I asked.

"The point is, I want you to understand that married people do have major disagreements. You weren't around for our early years. We had disagreements that left me so angry I would leave the house and drive around until I could calm down." Her tone was one of amused recollection.

I can picture this. Mom and I are both volatile. We are easily upset at times. We have both needed to find ways to blow off steam without decapitating those we love. I can see her driving that old Chevy around town.

"You and Mark are going to fight," she continued. "It's inevitable. I just don't want you to think that we had a smooth course. We didn't. We learned how to love. You will need to learn how to settle a disagreement in a reasonable way."

Mom must not think I am all that reasonable when angry. Imagine that!

I married Mark. I got frustrated with Mark. I took the car keys and stormed out of the apartment and drove around until I calmed down. I learned, with the patient tutelage of the Holy Spirit, how to settle a disagreement in a reasonable way.

And Mom's words and life shaped me. I learned I could be frustrated beyond words and still love Mark. I learned that I needed to take a quick walk or a short (or long) drive to keep myself from saying things that would hurt him. I also hurt Mark many times and learned how to ask for forgiveness.

The night my mother died, my sister and I wept as my father held her and poured out his heart. Over and over he kept saying, "You girls don't know. You can never know what an incredible woman your mother was." To this day, he is still in love with his Nancy.

So you see, even in death she mentored me. She gave me the model of a marriage. With his partner on the other side, Dad still held her hand and wept out her praises. My mother's mentoring provided the foundation for the person I have become.

MENTORS BASED ON NEED

By the grace of God, I have had other mentors besides Mom, women who have filled my life with their wisdom, their knowledge, their sense of fun. These women entered my life because of my needs. They had attributes I craved, and they were kind enough to come alongside and teach me from their own journeys.

Ernestine is a woman who has helped me become an adult, teaching me what it means to love God as an adult. She is the one who most often helps with the process. Ernestine knows the process.

I met Ernestine when I was twenty-three years old. She teaches the Word of God like a Bible professor. She has a passion for the written word that stabilizes me. Like me, Ernestine is a reader, and once we knew that about each other, the friendship was solid.

I believe we seek out mentors because they have in their lives an element we want. I sought out Ernestine because she had a depth in the Word of God that I wanted. She had walked out her faith in some pretty difficult circumstances and had maintained her love for the Savior. By my early thirties, I knew that life was going to hand all of us some pretty difficult circumstances, and I wanted stability like Ernestine's.

Ernestine would be the first to say she has not mentored me. I think the word *mentor* is intimidating to her, as it is for so many of us. Let me tell you a little about what Ernestine has done for me, and you can decide if she's a mentor or not.

Whenever my walk becomes difficult and I don't know what to do or where to turn, I end up in Ernestine's living room. She pours tea, hands out Kleenex, takes out the Scripture and reveals its wisdom.

When my mother lay dying, Ernestine prayed with me. She prayed for me. She listened. When I needed a day away from all of it, she talked about books and movies and children and never mentioned Mom at all. She was an oasis.

When I turned forty and Mom was gone, Ernestine asked what I wanted for my birthday. No party? No craziness? She arrived with my friends Wendy and Annie and made a lovely brunch. Together we sat and smiled and were still.

When my children have worn out my knees, she allows them to wear out hers. When I had surgery, when they thought I might die, she joined others who stormed heaven's gates and said, "No!" God heard their prayers.

She reads manuscripts and makes suggestions. She reads finished projects and applauds.

Ernestine would say we are just friends, and we are. But she is so much more. She is that woman who has walked farther, worked harder and knows Jesus better than I. She provides stability for me. She is the sister whose footsteps I look for, whose walk I follow.

And then there's Diane, my wonderful friend from Arkansas. Though I had taught a bit, speaking at retreats was new and daunting. Diane heard me fussing about this new arena the Lord had introduced into my life and stepped in to help me. "Girlfriend," she said with a laugh, "if you want to see what not to do, come follow me." I followed. Diane is my ideal when it comes to retreats: she can tell a story that will leave you laughing so hard it hurts. She loves the Lord and loves to laugh. I learned much about what to do and nothing about "what not to do."

The first retreat I followed Diane on was a jewel that I still treasure. With small children at home, just the idea of a weekend away was alluring. But Diane came up with the best plan: I was given the job of praying at the retreat. She had gone over her notes with me and I was to pray the entire time, sitting in the back. I was to pray that the Holy Spirit would do his deepest possible work in each life. I was to pray that Diane would stay on track. I was to pray that the women would have open hearts.

So I prayed and Diane preached. (I'm sorry. I know that, for many of us, women teach and do not preach, but women, she preached!) The Holy Spirit was present and lives were touched. Lives were changed. And in the midst of it all, at a moment when an issue came up that Diane knew I was writing about, that amazing teacher turned and gave me the floor. Just like that I got to practice in front of a pro.

I will never forget that moment. She smiled graciously and said, "You all know I travel with a friend who prays while we meet. This time it's Carol, and I happen to know that this is a question that Carol can answer best. The Lord has been talking to her about this very thing."

To say I was scared was an understatement. I was terrified. But Diane was smiling. And she was right: the question was on target. We had discussed that very issue on the drive down. I had poured out my heart to Diane, telling her all I had learned about it.

So Diane just turned the whole thing over to the novice, and you know what? The Holy Spirit was still present as Diane and I shifted jobs. She prayed, and for a brief time I taught. It was only for a few moments, but I taught—hadn't gotten to preaching yet—and lives were touched, lives were changed.

What an incredible woman! What generosity! She recognized that the Holy Spirit was present and that it was our job to get out of his way and let the work occur. But that is how Diane is. She is always interested in his work and never in hers. Her rule of thumb is this: We don't care who the Holy Spirit speaks through; we are just grateful that he speaks.

It is a rule that I strive to follow. The early church knew it. They all brought songs or verses to their gatherings and shared them. In today's culture, it is often one authority who speaks. A teacher or retreat speaker gets all the fun of being used by the Holy Spirit. Diane taught me that we need to learn to share the fun.

We often turn to women for help when they have qualities we seek. Sometimes they have a skill we want to acquire. Sometimes they have a character quality that we feel light-years away from obtaining. When we find the right person, our mentoring sessions tend to be more formal in nature. I watch Ernestine with a conscious intent to learn. I do the same with Diane and several others. These lessons are deliberate attempts to learn from my mentors.

INFORMAL MENTORS

There are other mentors whose presence in our lives is cherished and often unnoticed. These informal mentors are the women we work with on the job, in the church, in the raising of our children, in the loving of our husbands. They are often our peers. They are "just friends" whose impact in our lives is priceless.

Today, at the age of forty-five, I have several "best friends": Cathy has been a sister to my soul since college. Wendy feeds my artistic spirit. Debbie takes care of me, praying regularly for me and my children. Susan creates a home that renews me. Penny watches over my schedule and reminds me of the need for solid intellectual and emotional rest.

It is a wide and powerful circle. My children are growing up in the love of these additional "aunties." I am growing up in their love also.

Often our friends, our trusted lifelong friends, guide much of our growth. Dee Brestin refers to these friends as "perennials." I love that idea, because the plants that return to my garden each spring have become old friends. I look for their shoots to appear, nurture their growth, enjoy their beauty. Annuals are lovely, put perennials are relationship and character builders.

One of my perennials is my college roommate, Cathy. Her husband, Bob, serves our country as a military man with great passion and integrity. Our children trace their understanding of U.S. geography and history to the places Uncle Bob and Aunt Cathy have lived. They have lived all over the nation, and today they are based in Hong Kong.

Cathy and I have found it necessary to visit each other wherever we are. Bob sent a ticket to me two years ago to make sure I visited them in China. It somehow helps to have a visual idea of each other's surroundings. I love knowing where the international school is and where the boys catch their bus. I can still recall the smells of the wet market and the glory of the flower stalls.

Last spring, Cathy came to visit me. She had not seen this house, though I have lived here four years. We laughed, talked, shopped, talked, talked and, well, visited until all hours for one week. It was a busy week. I had much going on at work. My schedule was a bit crazy, and by Thursday night, Cathy was concerned. When the last kid was off doing homework, she suggested we visit out in the garden. We grabbed pillows and headed out into the warm night.

"Carol, this schedule has to stop," she said, just moments into the conversation.

I smiled, feeling that she just didn't understand my life. I had no intention of pursuing this conversation. "It will end. I promise. I'll be all rested by summer's end," I said.

"Don't do that," she urged. "Don't refuse to look at it realistically. You had surgery just nine months ago. Didn't that teach you anything?"

That hurt. The surgery had been terrifying. The doctors thought it was ovarian cancer. It wasn't, but the threat had been far too real. And I had learned. At least, I thought I had.

"Carol, that was not a blip on the screen," Cathy told me. "That was God getting your attention. You have to slow down."

I looked at the flowers and sighed. "Do we have to do this?" I asked.

"Yes, sweetie, we do. You won't know your own children if you keep up this pace."

Ouch. My children are my treasure. I can't bear it when I hurt them. I don't want to be told I'm not being a good mom.

Cathy hugged me and suggested we look at the schedule and try to make some adjustments. She knew I was hurting, but she knew she was right. Scripture says, "Wounds from a friend can be trusted" (Proverbs 27:6). My schedule was overloaded. I needed to make cuts. I needed more time to mother my kids. And I needed my friend to help me see it.

Cathy is loyal to the core, but her loyalty does not blind her. She knows my faults, knows I tend to overbook my life. She loves me enough to force the issue on occasion. She loves me enough to tell me the truth of a situation. She loves me enough to let me see her faults too. And so now, in our forties, with both our mothers inside heaven's gate, we teach each other. We teach gently, lovingly and firmly. We care for each other's souls.

What It's Like to Mentor

It is a wonderful thing to be mentored, yet it is difficult to be asked to mentor. Most of us do not feel able to teach. We are aware of our own flaws before God's throne and are afraid we might pass those imperfections on.

Naomi knew that difficulty. She had the same hesitation many of us feel when we are asked to mentor. Imagine what it must have been like for her. She and her husband had left Israel during a time of famine. They moved to the country of Moab, and there her husband died. Her sons took foreign wives, and later they also died.

C. S. Lewis tells us, "Grief is like the sky; it covers everything." To traverse that emotional landscape alone would be doubly painful. Yet that is what Naomi set out to do. She wanted to be alone with her grief.

One daughter-in-law refused to part with her. Ruth was adamant. She would stay with Naomi; she would make Naomi's home her own. Naomi's God would be her God, and she would be buried in Naomi's land. What a testimony of love between two women!

So Naomi returned home with a daughter of the heart. You can imagine how difficult this would have been for her. Have you ever been so low you had nothing to give? Certainly that was Naomi's life. She was depleted. She had lost everything, and she was bitter. Yet here was this young woman, needing her love, needing her help. Here was Ruth, a daughter of the heart who needed an introduction to the God of Israel.

Naomi found the strength to love. She gave direction. She watched God move.

God did bless these two. Naomi's God became Ruth's. Naomi's kinsman became Ruth's husband. And Ruth's child became Naomi's laughter.

It is easy to see the end of Naomi's story and to forget her blunt refusal to mentor Ruth. We forget that she asked Ruth to return home. We also spend little time considering the emotional reserves it took for Naomi to bring Ruth back to Israel. It cost Naomi something to teach and look after Ruth. She worried over her future. She fussed over Ruth, and she made mistakes of her own. She was human.

When we are asked to be special friends with younger women, it is easy to let the circumstances of our own lives crowd them out. We suggest they return to the church, find someone older, someone wiser. I have been known to say, "I don't know how to mentor."

I'll never forget telling one young woman just that. But she was tenacious. She informed me that we didn't need a format; she just wanted to "hang out." I am a child of the seventies, so hanging out is my forte. I let her know that my house was always open for hanging out. So that is what we did and what we still do. We talk while I iron. We laugh while I cook. We groan when the dryer buzzes. We learn from each other over the chores of daily life. As for who is mentoring whom, I'm well aware of what *I'm* learning: it doesn't take much to mentor if you like to hang out. Even my flaws, wrapped around the ironing board, are visible, recognizable and forgivable because of her kind heart.

The process changed us both, but did I become a mentor? Oh, I don't know. It's such a big word. I'm just in my forties, you know. Mentor? I think not. I think we just became friends.

FOR REFLECTION AND DISCUSSION

1. Who have been mentors to you? What do they bring to your life? What important lessons or skills have they taught you?

2. Read Titus 2. Consider your place in the circle of life. What do you need to learn? Who could mentor you? Consider the younger women in your life. What skills or character qualities do you have that you could help them develop?

3. Think about the ways other women have mentored you. How have they become part of your life? Was it formal? Informal? Did you ask for help? As you reflect on question two, how will you approach these women to ask for help or to offer it?

The Dance of Mentoring

. . . .

Jesus loved Martha and her sister and Lazarus.

JOHN 11:5

SARA'S STORY

Hurry up with that dough. Knead it thoroughly," Aunt Martha orders. I watch her from the corner of my eye, my hands deep in the flour and dough. My mother has sent me to Aunt Martha, asking her to teach me to cook. Cooking is a skill that has eluded my mother, but happily for her, my father employs a cook.

I often wonder why she didn't just let the cook teach me, but Mom is nothing if not stubborn. She said Aunt Martha would teach me more about cooking in a week than our cook could teach me in a lifetime. So here I sit, getting orders from my bossy Aunt Martha.

"Sara, knead that dough!" Aunt Martha's voice is commanding as she leaves the kitchen to attend to another chore. My hands resume their work. Aunt Martha's kitchen is rich in fine aromas. It smells of nutmeg and cinnamon. I look at the deep, gold color of the walls and sigh with contentment. All my cousins have been sent to Aunt Martha's home to learn cooking. It is a rite of passage for us—the family motto for women being "Beauty is lovely and character is fine, but a woman who can bake bread, she will be praised!"

Aunt Martha is a contradiction. Bossy. I swear I've never met a bossier woman in all my life. At the same time, she is the first to wrap me in her arms when I fail—the first to give me a sweet when I cry.

"Sara, there is a reason for the kneading," Aunt Martha begins. I had not seen her return, but now she is at my shoulder, all teacher again. "You need to get the salt and yeast evenly distributed throughout the dough. Not too much, or the bread is tough. It needs to be soft and springy," she instructs. Aunt Martha's hands take over my chore, and within minutes the dough is the consistency she described. Even my untrained hands can sense the magic she is working. It is soft and springy.

"Can't I just use a spoon?" I ask, trying to make this daily chore easier.

"No," she answers with a smile. "I asked my own mother the same question and the answer is the same. Every one of your cousins has asked it. You can't use a spoon."

"Have you always known how to cook, Aunt Martha?" I ask.

"I love to cook. I love to feed a big group and watch them relax over the food. It's just who I am. A very funny part of who I am.

"You think I don't know I am bossy?" She laughs. I have the grace to blush. "I know I am bossy. I want the meal to be more than just food. I want it to be medicine to tired people. I want them to sit down at my table and know they are special. I want them to relax and shed the weight of the day. It takes work to do that." She sighs, pulling the dough from the table and setting it to rise again.

"I don't know if I will ever love running a home the way you do," I admit. I want to learn but I cannot see myself as my Aunt Martha. She knows how to do everything. She knows how to make bread and wine, arrange flowers and entertain large groups. She is still smiling when they leave her house. She whistles while she cleans up the mess. I like the excitement of company, but I have never wanted to be the one serving others. I like being served!

"Aunt Martha," I begin, my voice taking on the tones of confession. "I don't think I will ever serve people the way you do. I think I am a little selfish."

She dries her hands. Her eyes are smiling, crinkling up at the corners, and her mouth is working hard to control her grin. "Sara, do you want to love or just to be loved?" she asks.

It is a difficult question. She is waiting for an answer.

"I want to love," I say, "but I also want to be loved." The room is quiet as she cleans the table.

"Well, sweet Sara, you are like every other human being I know. We all want to be loved. We just get the order confused. We want to love out of the abundance of being loved. Jesus was not like that, Sara. He loved first and he loved generously. He loved me when I was having fits over kitchen help and he loved me when Lazarus was in the tomb. He loved me when I doubted him and he loved me when I believed.

"I think it was that generous love that taught me to love. I finally learned how to just love and not worry about the outcome. After all, Jesus would always love me. He knew me better than I know myself, and he loved me."

I think about that. Being loved even when I am not lovely. My mom loves me like that, mostly. She gets angry with me, but she loves me. I wonder about Aunt Martha. She is bossy, but she sure does love me. She sure loves Aunt Mary and Uncle Lazarus. She loves all those noisy men who come to eat and share Sabbath.

"Sara." She nudges my arm. "Let's start on the vegetables."

. . . .

THE SEARCH FOR MENTORS

We all want a mentor. We want someone to show us how to live and how to love. We want to know everything, from how to bake bread to how to love a difficult child. We were created to live in community, and it is in community that we frequently learn our most valuable lessons.

Often the easiest place to connect with a mentor is in the area of life skills. Many of us have specialized knowledge that is easy and fun to share. Asking simple questions about a skill that eludes us can be a direct route into a mentoring relationship. Being available to answer those questions and to discuss the process of quilting, baking, gardening, writing or a host of other desired skills is often how we hook up with women we mentor and who in turn mentor us.

I grew up in an era that was poised between a fifties understanding of women and their place in the home and a seventies understanding of a liberated woman—which means I grew up confused! There were elements of homemaking that appealed to me and elements of vocation that called to me. I wanted the best of both worlds and had only twenty-four hours in my day.

The Chinese say that when the student is ready, the teacher will come. I find that proverb to be true in my life. As I grew ready to learn, a teacher arrived. That's because we seek out a teacher only when there is a skill or character quality that needs to be developed in our own repertoire.

When Mark and I married in 1983, I knew how to make a mean macaroni and cheese (Kraft) and how to iron my clothes. My father had grown up during the Depression, and his childhood was full of work. His desire was that his daughters grow up without much work. My mother acquiesced, and I grew up happy, carefree and ignorant of the process of keeping a home.

Mom did much to help me during those first years of marriage. She taught me that love is often expressed in small favors. She taught me that Mark would probably like to come home and not have to teach me to cook. She told me that anyone can read a cookbook. She was adamant that love is expressed in how we live, not just in kisses at the doorway.

Just about the time I got the hang of modest cooking, I had three children in less than three years. I then needed a mentor in mothering. My own mother had become a grandmother, and the first thing I learned about grandmothers is that they do not resemble their former selves. My children could do no wrong in my mother's eyes. I needed help from someone who knew that my beautiful babies were real human beings. The Lord graciously sent my friend Wendy.

Wendy is one of those women who are natural nurturers. She loves small children and has a wonderful way of making them feel accepted, loved and special. My children adore her. Today they are fifteen, sixteen and seventeen, and they still require regular "Wendy fixes." Wendy's farm is a haven for them, and her spirit is a safe place for all of us. We live about thirty minutes away from her, and yet Megan, a senior this year, insisted on having her senior pictures taken at Wendy's farm. "Mom, I grew up there!" she exclaimed. I often feel that our whole family grew up on Wendy's farm.

I've had other friends who have filled other voids. Karen and Debra taught me to cook. They deserve awards for perseverance. Both took very basic skills and showed me new ways to make meals that would "wow" my family. They searched out simple recipes with fantastic presentation and made me look good on special occasions. They laughed and giggled and swallowed back hysterics while watching me try.

Susan has a home I love to enter. A nurse for years, she creatively runs a beautiful and orderly home. I have never walked into her house to find chaos. Her home is a sanctuary. Susan listened to me when I expressed envy of her home. She heard me lament my own disorderly ways and my frustrations with three teenagers, three dogs and a host of visitors. Finally she asked what my own processes were. Processes? I was ashamed to say that I did my piece and was often found yelling to get others to do their jobs. Susan said that most of what I did was fine, but she did have one trick that would save me years of frustration. I was ready to learn!

The concept is the five-minute swoosh. A run through the house before bed allows me to pick up any mess and wake up to a clean house. I cannot begin to tell you the difference this makes. I have never been an easy riser. To wake up to a clean, orderly home makes a huge difference in my outlook. And Susan is right. It usually only takes about five minutes to restore order before I go to bed.

Other areas of my life have needed instruction. Vocation is one. As my children began their journey through adolescence, I began a journey of my own. I had loved teaching as a young woman and had spent about ten years out of the classroom. Once my children were out of the toddler stage, I returned to the classroom to substitute teach. This allowed me to keep my hand in the profession while providing our family with additional income.

With children entering their teens, I returned to school to earn a master's degree and began the road back to the vocation that had never stopped singing her siren song. I earned the master's and began to do some part-time teaching at George Fox University in Portland. During that time, I sought advice from several sources as I contemplated working toward a doctorate in education. This would allow me to continue teaching at the university, a job I had grown to love. It would also be a strain on my family.

One of the people I spoke with was Dr. Grace Balwit. Grace has raised a family and remains very attached to her children and grandchildren. She also enjoys teaching and is active in her field. We talked about the role of mentor I was playing, both consciously and unconsciously. We talked about how, believing that we are created in the image of God, it is important to follow those vocational paths that we believe God is calling us to. She reminded me that the children would be encouraged to follow God's leading by the example I set. I had looked only at the disadvantages; she helped me see the overall plan.

My children added their voices to this decision. They argued that I was a bit too attached to them. With all three leaving home in the next four years, they thought my vocational call was straight from God. They rejoiced in the breathing room it would provide them.

Today I teach full time at the university, training individuals who wish to enter the teaching profession. I am also working, very slowly, on my doctorate, with another two-plus years before I finish. My children love my job and the exposure to the university it provides them. I am full of the joy of a great vocation. My husband is pleased for me and finds that my reentry into his profession has revitalized his own work.

Grace and others helped me make a decision that benefits many, including my family. She was a spiritual and professional mentor who knew what it meant to love one's work but to desire a healthy, happy family first. She helped me understand that I can have a richly rewarding career while living at a pace slow enough to accommodate my family.

ME? TEACH LIFE SKILLS?

It is all very well to sing the praises of those who mentor us. It is an easy thing to do. A right thing to do. But it is difficult to look inside and recognize the life skills we have that others can learn from.

Three years ago I began to look among the many wonderful formal mentoring programs to find one for our church to use. Our women's commission decided we wanted to run a version of Betty Huizenga's Apples of Gold, a six-week mentoring program in which the older women share life skills with the younger women. It includes lessons on six topics: loving your husband, loving your children, purity, submission and hospitality, with a gourmet cooking lesson followed by a wonderful meal at each session. Everyone was quite excited until we read the fine print, which stated that the women I had recruited to teach would be mentoring other women.

The reality was that none of us was all that comfortable with the mentoring part. We are in our early to late forties. (We have very few older women in our church.) All but one of us still have children at home. We did not see ourselves in the mentoring role. Not yet.

So we had to work it through. Think about it, talk about it and pray about it. We finally agreed that we could teach the lessons, but the part about being a mentor . . . well, maybe we could just be friends with these women, who were not all that much younger than us.

By the end of the six weeks, I had watched Jesus at work. Woman after woman stated that she had learned much. The teachers learned as much as the women who came to learn. Every one of us grew. Every one of us developed deeper friendships. We all found people we could run to for prayer or advice or who would refer us to Scripture.

We were changed.

We have run the program twice now and have a waiting list for next year's workshop. We are also developing a program for mothers of adolescents, which we are calling Settings of Silver. This will include the cooking lessons as well as spiritual lessons about making your home the center of adolescent life, launching your children, keeping your marriage alive as you enter an empty nest and returning to the workplace.

We are also planning to launch Apple Seeds, a program that will teach women ages eighteen to twenty-eight the basics of cooking and the spiritual lessons of self-image, finances, purity and community building. Women in their thirties will run this program.

These workshops are formal settings with a relaxed atmosphere and lots of laughter. Friendships form and lives connect. We have had profound experiences during our times together. I am constantly amazed at the spiritual depths of our discussions, often beginning with a woman wanting to learn how to cook a heart-healthy meal. While teaching how to make salsa, we had a woman meet Jesus for the first time. Imagine, tomatoes and Jesus. What an introduction into the kingdom of God! This is the reality of mentoring. It takes the ordinary and weds it to the eternal.

Mentoring is really about being a true friend. It is recognizing that you have a skill or an insight that is of value to another woman. I do not believe that we are called to just mentor or be mentored. It is not an either-or situation. It is hospitality of the heart.

Who can you assist on her journey? How can you be hospitable? What skills do you have that a woman five years younger than you might need? Who oohed and ahhed over your last dessert? Who wants to know how you painted your kitchen? Who has just started working again and needs some help learning the ropes?

And who has a skill or character trait that you crave?

If we are to be truly hospitable, we must begin in the heart. We must reveal our lives, our skills, our weaknesses to those we trust and begin the process of learning from each other. We must embrace a hospitality of the heart and recognize it as mentoring and being mentored in return.

FOR REFLECTION AND DISCUSSION

1. Name three skills you have developed. (These can be anything from sponge painting, to traveling abroad, to sticking with a budget.) How can these skills be used to strengthen the body of Christ?

2. Name three skills you crave. Who has these skills? Have you asked that person for help?

3. Read Romans 12:9-13. Think now of those who have taught you or mentored you. How can you express your gratitude to them? How can you honor those in your circle who have helped you on your own spiritual journey?

Convert My Heart

. . . .

When a woman who had lived a sinful life in that town learned that Jesus was eating at the Pharisee's house, she brought an alabaster jar of perfume, and as she stood behind him at his feet weeping, she began to wet his feet with her tears.

LUKE 7:37-38

MARY'S STORY

I grew up in a household of whores. My father schooled us well, and we grew up knowing that all women are whores. My brothers were allowed to use my sisters as they chose. I was spared some of that because I was an unusually beautiful child—one whose virginity would bring a good price.

On my eleventh birthday, my father sold my virginity to a man who paid well and had use of me for three days. He took me and taught me the art of the flesh.

Returning home, my brothers made their living off my body. I learned my lessons well and fetched high prices. And while men pretended I was a body without a soul, an object to be used, I learned to deceive. To fake pleasure. To hide my murderous rage.

I became so good at the deception I fooled myself. By the time I was sixteen I no longer felt anger. I no longer felt anything.

When I turned twenty, my brothers chose new prey. A prophet had come to town. A man of God. Men of God can sometimes be my best clients. They pay once for the pleasure and then pay many times for my silence.

We went to hear the prophet preach, my brothers and I. He was like any other. A common-looking fellow with a band of men who jockeyed for positions near him.

The setting was a common one, but the words were different. They were spoken by an innocent. Words that spoke of a kindness I did not know existed. Words of blessing. Of the meek inheriting the earth. Of the poor in spirit inheriting the kingdom of God.

I began to squirm. I did not want to seduce this one. I began to question my ability to do so. I had trouble looking this one in the eyes.

And then he captured my eyes with his and said these words: "Blessed are the pure in heart, for they shall see God."

It was as if he had reached inside my soul and grasped my heart in his hand. I felt wrung out. Exposed. The pain of my lifestyle, the devastation of my whoring, could no longer be hidden from my eyes.

It was three days before the healing took place. The prophet stayed in town, preaching to crowds. I stayed at home, locked in my rooms, contemplating his words. Finally, on his last night in town, I went to the Pharisee's house.

The prophet was meeting with the religious leaders. They were reclining at the table. And I joined them.

Simon, in whose home they ate, moved to remove me, but one look into the prophet's eyes had him lowering himself back to the table. The prophet turned, gentle eyes questioning mine.

Words deserted me, and the tears that had not left my eyes since my eleventh birthday forced their way up my chest and into my throat.

Unpinning my hair, I knelt behind him, seeking to avoid the kindness in his eyes. Convulsive tears washed the dust from his feet. I took my hair and gently, with a love and tenderness I had never given expression, wiped those feet dry.

Somewhere outside this epiphany, I heard the teacher and Simon exchanging words. The words were useless to me. This man's eyes . . . his nod . . . his words. They were bathing me, cleansing me, just as I now cleansed his feet.

Finally, my job done, I took a costly perfume and poured it on his feet. Others would anoint his head. They had earned the right to such a privilege. I would anoint those beautiful feet and be proud of the honor.

The talk at the table stilled. Turning to me, the prophet smiled. There was no lust in his smile. My hair, disheveled and alluring, did not lure him. "Your sins are forgiven," he whispered.

He had known! He was forgiving!

"Your faith has saved you; go in peace."

I stumbled to my feet brand-new. Born again. Made whole. The whore was gone. Wholeness had replaced that shattered place forever.

. . . .

SALVATION

Webster's says that *salvation* is "the act of being saved from danger, evil, difficulty, destruction. Rescue from the consequences of sin." For believers, salvation is a one-time event that involves the surrender of our lives into the control of Jesus Christ. It is a moment in time when we are birthed into the realm of the eternal, the kingdom of God.

Today, some two thousand years after Jesus ascended to the Father, most of us come to know him by spending time with others who know him. We meet Jesus by meeting his family. We find him first in the faces of those who love him.

It is in these faces that we find mentors. In many ways, these mentors become spiritual midwives. They lead us into the kingdom of God and are there when we draw our first eternal breath.

I love it when women with children get together. Sooner or later, birthing stories are shared, stories of long, painful labors, stories of compassionate midwives, stories of quick trips that ended with a birth in the back seat of a car. Our stories bind us together as sisters, as members of the same family. We are a community of birth moms.

While many men shake their heads over the repetition of these stories, it seems to me a profound sharing. We are sharing a temporal experience that completely consumed us—body, soul and spirit. We are sharing an experience that allowed us to partner with God in the act of creation.

Salvation is very much like birth. Jesus calls it being born again. For those of us who have been privileged to midwife such a birth, it is every bit as emotional, as consuming, as when our own children were born. So, when women who love Jesus get together, sooner or later the stories of salvation begin to flow—just like the stories of labor. We recall the child we prayed over for a decade. We remember the neighbor who dropped to her knees in our kitchen. Over and over, with tears and with laughter, we recall the stories of birth—of being born again.

REBIRTH AS A CHILD

My own experience with salvation began with Mom in 1966, when I was eight years old and becoming quite inventive with my storytelling. Apparently I had told one too many stories and Mom was determined to straighten out my erring ways.

Mom was about to mentor me into a salvation experience. We sat on the couch, next to the avocado-green hi-fi. She told me that not only was she unhappy with my lie, but that Jesus was too. She talked to me about how hard it is to stop something like lying. She told me she could only stop her own temper when Jesus came to live in her heart. She said that having Jesus in her heart helped her.

I remember playing with my fingernails. Pushing the cuticles back and forth with my teeth. Letting her words wash over me. Adjusting to the idea that Mom had her own battles to fight. That she seemed to need the help of Jesus to win them.

"Think I need Jesus too?" I asked, fairly certain of her response.

"I do," she said.

"How do we get him?"

"We pray. This way." And there on the couch, next to the avocado-green hi-fi, I made my way into the kingdom of God. Haltingly. Taking deep breaths, for even an eight-year-old knows when something important is happening. The Savior, hearing my words, knowing that I wanted his influence and help, came and made me a child of the King.

Mom called Dad into the living room. He came and lay down on the floor near the couch. "Tell Dad what you just did," Mom said.

I was tongue-tied. One of the only times in my life, but tongue-tied nonetheless. You see, something intensely personal had just happened. I felt all new inside. I felt fragile and uncertain. I felt very much like a newborn.

For me, that was salvation. A birth. A new identity. Forever owned by One who could be trusted above all others. Encouraged and led by my mother. Rejoiced over by my father. And partied over by angels.

As my own babies grew, I became anxious to partner with God in their lives. I did not think of it as mentoring, but I sure thought of it as partnering. I knew that I could do nothing to secure their second birth. There could be no pushing. I could only nurture, listening closely to their questions and encouraging their love of God.

At the age of four, Megan wanted Jesus in her heart. She spoke to her daddy about it, and Mark promptly prayed with her. On his knees, he was privileged to see his eldest born into the realm of the eternal. He did not question her; he simply knew what she was asking and made sure he did all he could to help her find her way into the Savior's arms.

Days later, three-year-old Rachael was tugging at my leg. "Mama, I want Jesus too!" she demanded.

I smiled at the sweet package of joy. Smiled at her open heart and at her eagerness. Then I made the mental decision that she was too young for a second birth. You see, I'm the nurturer in the family. I was determined that each stage of child development be followed. I wanted her to understand it all, and I was going to make sure she did before she prayed.

"Rachael, honey, just what exactly do you want from Jesus?" I asked, dropping down on the floor to her level. There, on the kitchen floor, she arranged her plump little legs.

"I want Jesus to come into my heart too!" she proclaimed, accepting no nonsense from her mother.

"And I'm sure he wants to come in," I said, willing to leave this holy moment and go on to other things. I was confident that if Mark and I thought four was young, three was not workable. Too soon. Premature. Observing her outward growth, I had determined that her heart was too young. I was not willing to midwife this birth. I thought it too early.

God, who delights in those so fresh from his creative hand, had other plans.

"Mommy!" Rachael said, her voice commanding. "Don't we pray now? Megan and Daddy prayed and then Jesus came to live in Megan's heart. Aren't you going to pray with me?"

Check. There was no escape this time. So we would pray, I decided. She could pray it again later—when she really understood.

This would just be a preview. "Sure, Rachael honey. We can pray."

So we knelt by the children's play table, hands folded ever so correctly, and Rachael asked Jesus to come into her heart. At three years old, she asked him to be her Savior.

I began to think this small event might be the real thing. What if she did understand, on some level, this need for Jesus? What if he was more real to her than I realized? What if a birth had just occurred and I had been playing pretend?

I hugged my wee one and returned to the stove to begin dinner. Five or six minutes passed before the chubby hand of a three-year-old was once again tugging at my leg. "Mommy, aren't we gonna have a party?" she asked, looking expectant.

"A party?" I asked, completely dumbfounded.

"Yes, Mommy. A birthday party. See, now I am born into God's family and Daddy said all the angels in heaven would get happy and excited and throw a big party. Don't we get to come?"

Her inquiring face is frozen in time for me. A birthday party. A three-year-old who knew that she had just been born of God. A mommy who needed to play catch-up real fast. And a tender Lord, gracious enough to let a fumbling mother play midwife.

Little Rachael. She was born three weeks early on earth. She was right on time for eternity. Nothing premature about this birth. Today she is fifteen. She loves Jesus with all her heart. She has not needed to revisit salvation; she has always been secure with her eternal birth.

COMMITTEES OF MIDWIVES AND MENTORS

Not everyone finds Jesus as a child. Childhood is an easy time to find him, because as children we have not yet lost our understanding of the miraculous. As adults, we like to think we can explain it all. Children know instinctively that magic happens. And there is no stronger magic than the creative power of Jesus Christ who, by a nod of his head, can change me from temporal to eternal. Miraculous.

As adults, we often need to be loved to Jesus. We need a circle of midwives and mentors. You know how that works. One sister tells another of a need, a group of women come together and meet that need, and relationships are formed. Sometime, after months of sharing and loving, someone is invited to meet Jesus. And because love is the avenue, it is easier to make that long walk down the aisle.

Yvonne did not find Jesus as a child. She had a difficult childhood and early adulthood. By the time she met Jesus, she had built up reservoirs of anger and bitterness. Living with her sister, a member of a charismatic church, she "wasn't going to have anything to do with those tongues-talking, hand-raising women!" Their enthusiasm fueled her anger. Happily her anger did not discourage those women. They decided to love her to Jesus.

One in particular made Yvonne her personal challenge. In her home one day, Doris laid down the gauntlet. Taking Yvonne's face in her hands, she said, "I'm gonna love you no matter what!" And love her she did.

Doris worked in a shoe store, a few blocks away from Yvonne's job. Yvonne had very little in the way of material goods. Doris had a little bit more, although neither had much.

Doris began to notice the needs in Yvonne's life. Yvonne returned from lunch one day to find a new pair of shoes on her desk—a gift from Doris, who knew Yvonne liked them. Then there was the time Doris took the watch off her wrist and gave it to Yvonne. There were notes and hugs, lunches and a quiet spirit that was willing to listen to all of the anger and just keep loving Yvonne.

Finally, two years into Doris's loving project, Yvonne met Jesus. The women had met at her sister's home on New Year's Eve. Yvonne hid in the bedroom as those tongues-talking, hand-raising women prayed and praised in the living room. Finally Yvonne could not stand her anger. She rushed into the living room and cried, "I don't want to be like this anymore!" Arms enfolded her, tears joined her own, and a group of tongues-talking, hand-raising women led this hurt woman to the Healer.

Yvonne has walked with Jesus ever since. When she tells the story, her eyes dance and she laughs a great deal. But when she speaks of Doris, her eyes fill. "She has never stopped loving me," Yvonne says. "Never." It's a quality of midwives, that never-ending love. It's a quality of the Savior who brings eternal life.

My own grandparents were loved to Jesus. In an era when so much preaching was given over to hellfire and damnation, a small community in North Dakota loved my grandma and grandpa into the kingdom of God. When they lost their farm during the Depression, the community moved these two young adults and their five, soon to be six, children into town. They lived with a family, learned to pray with that family. My aunts tell me that three years later, when someone finally asked Grandma if she wouldn't like to give her life to Jesus, she was on her knees before they finished the sentence. Yes, Grandma was loved to Jesus, shown his love in tangible ways and introduced to him with loving words.

Constantly Converting the Heart

Growing up, I thought salvation was a one-time event. You prayed, asked Jesus into your heart and life, and experienced salvation. I remember clearly my first indication that salvation might entail more in my life as a believer than I had thought as a child.

I was about twenty-six years old when those thought patterns were challenged. A speaker at our church talked about the need to be "constantly converting the heart of the believer." The phrases bothered me deeply. After all, I could point to a place in time when the event of salvation had occurred in my life.

I spoke to Ernestine, my favorite teacher and mentor, after the service. "Ernestine, what did he mean? Constantly converting the heart? Aren't our hearts converted at salvation? Isn't salvation a one-time thing?"

Ernestine smiled without any condescension—how does she do it? "Carol, of course your heart was converted at salvation. Certainly salvation is given as a gift. But Scripture also says to work out your salvation with fear and trembling. Doesn't that suggest that here on earth there might be some work to do? Don't you think there are areas of our hearts that resist conversion? Areas that hide from the light?"

"Hummm . . . okay, I get it," I said, anxious to get away. I wanted to forget this concept. I did not want to examine the areas of my heart that were choosing to stay away from conversion. Ernestine let me go, and waited. Over the next decade she would find me at her doorstep again and again, needing help. Discoveries of sin-encrusted areas of my life would continue to haunt me, and it was often Ernestine who would gently discuss the implications, love me into confession and help me find a new path.

THE CONTINUAL NEED FOR A SAVIOR

Today I continue to recognize my ongoing need for God to work out salvation in various areas in my life. Several years ago I found myself in a twelve-step group for overeaters. I, who thought I had all the answers, had hit a wall. God used this experience to teach me a valuable lesson. There are areas of my life that desperately needed a savior. And the only Savior I know is the only Savior capable of fixing me. Of converting my stubborn little heart. Of saving me. Repeatedly.

My fluctuating weight is a trustworthy barometer of my surrender to the Savior. If I am carrying extra weight, there is an area in my life that I am wrestling with. An area that needs either the anesthetizing effect of food or the touch of the Savior. My constant battle with weight reminds me that I often choose an anesthetic rather than the difficult but purifying process of ongoing salvation.

LeAnn was in my twelve-step group. She had struggled with weight from her childhood. And believe me, weight was all any of us had on our agenda. LeAnn and I talked often of our need for a savior. When I realized that was my need, I began to speak of it often—daily praying for his salvation in this bothersome area of my life.

LeAnn spent six weeks on step one. Step one is the most obnoxious step in all twelve-step programs. In it you admit that your life is out of control and you desperately need a higher power. "It's interesting to think about step one," LeAnn says. "My biggest struggle is being willing to need a savior."

Today LeAnn lives in a small town ten minutes from me. She raises chickens, homeschools four children, runs a cleaning service and works harder than anyone I know. This woman is one of the gems of Christendom, not because she works so hard, but because she works at converting her stubborn heart.

Having grown up in a legalistic church community, LeAnn knows the law like a Bible professor. And when she talks of the work God has done in her life as an adult, she is willing to confess that all she wanted was for her life to be totally together. Together so that anyone could see any part of it and know it was right. That was all. All she wanted was a beautiful facade.

"But that was never on God's agenda, Carol," she explains to me. "God was only concerned about converting my heart to his ways. He didn't need to build a fancy picture window. He wanted to build a real home. A home where he could roam freely, examining rooms and changing things. He didn't care about public appearances."

LeAnn and I smile. She knows that I would also like wonderful public appearances—never mind the mess in the next room. LeAnn has known me and cared for me with a stubbornness I find reassuring. She knows the areas I try to hide. I know the areas she tries to hide. Regardless, the love and respect continue. We are sisters for the long haul.

"You know, " she continues, "Christianity without the daily Savior is just another religion."

"Yes. And a pretty demanding religion at that," I say with a laugh.

"God has never been interested in my competence," LeAnn says. "I hated that I had to ask God to help me. I was raised on a farm. You learn to be independent. It is still hard for me to accept that it is the needy who God comes to.

"You can take a long time to come to your own neediness. I had known Jesus as Savior since the tenth grade. Now I know him as my daily Savior—at thirty-six. It took me a long time to try all the other alternatives. It takes a while to get cornered, but thank God he does corner us. He lets us get needy so that we can experience again his salvation."

LeAnn's words ring through my psyche. "It is the needy who God comes to . . . only the needy."

I also think about my friend Lori. She came from a very legalistic background too, and her bottom line was that she never wanted to get in trouble with God. "Twenty years of trying to please God on my own and I failed miserably," Lori says. "I never knew his love or his mercy or his grace. Finding out that I daily need a savior has paved the way for God to become a personal friend and Lord instead of a far-off deity. Now I can leave the marble throne room of God's judgment and climb onto his lap and call him Daddy."

MENTORS WHO GUIDE

It is the mentors, the sisters of faith in my life who teach me the truths of salvation. They remind me that out of the daily details of our lives the Savior comes and works the miraculous. When I am discouraged or worried, these same mentors come and we share birthing stories. We share stories of earthly babies and eternal children of God. We share stories of daily redemption and of our need for a savior. We revisit salvation together, making daily inroads into the depths of his teaching. We make progress as mentors and mentorees. We find ourselves converted into his likeness, a little more each day.

FOR REFLECTION AND DISCUSSION

1. What is your personal experience with salvation?

2. Who has mentored you in the area of salvation? What has he or she taught you about being born again?

3. Scripture speaks of working out your salvation and growing up in your salvation (see Philippians 2:12-13 and 1 Peter 2:1-3). What do these verses say? What qualities do they instruct us to have? What areas of your life need the saving hand of God? Who has character qualities you lack? Would they be open to mentoring you? Have you asked them?

Teach Me to Pray

. . . .

There was also a prophetess, Anna, the daughter of Phanuel, of the tribe of Asher. . . . She never left the temple but worshiped night and day, fasting and praying.

LUKE 2:36-37

ANNA'S STORY

One young mother came back alone. Her work was finished, her son properly dedicated at the temple. "Anna," she says, her voice soft and melodic. "Anna, how do I pray?"

The question is asked often of me, now that I am eighty-four years old. How do you pray? I often think that if they understood how prayer is forged, they would refuse to pray. "Mary, child," I answer, "prayer is simple, but praying is hard work. Learning to pray is forged in a very hot fire . . . one that often takes your life away."

The young mother looks confused. This is not the message she has come to hear. I entreat, "Let me tell you how I learned to pray." The young Mary falls quiet, listening carefully to me. "At your age, I was like any other young girl. I had a handsome husband, one who loved me and one who had every corner of my heart. Oh, Jonathan was a wonderful man. We lived together seven years, and I have never wanted another. How could I? I had lived with heaven. Anything less would have been a grave disappointment.

"One summer, my mother fell ill. Being her only child, it fell to me to nurse her. I loved Mama, and that summer was the hardest of my life. I watched her waste away. The flesh disappeared from her frame, and by harvest, Mama was skin and bones. She was in constant pain, and her grimaces and moans left me crazy with grief. I begged God to take her, commanded God to take her. But it seemed that God was not listening.

"Then, during the heat of the harvest, Jonathan fell in the fields.

"I have never had a time like that, before or since. Mama would not die, but Jonathan was gone before they could bring him to our home."

Mary's eyes fill with tears. Seeing the tears, I think this is good. If she is to mother this one, she will need her tender heart. I will have to remember to pray that it is as strong as it is tender. "Mary, it is good you should cry," I say. "Men like my Jonathan, like your Joseph, they are rare, child. Love like that is rare.

"My mama died the day after we buried Jonathan." My voice wavers with old tears.

Silence stretches out. I do not realize I have become lost in the memory of those days until Mary's arm encircles my waist. "Mother Anna, it is enough," she whispers. "You do not have to tell me more."

Wiping my eyes, I smile. "No child. It is not enough. You need to learn to pray and I need to tell you how I learned. The story will be helpful to you one day." The prophet in me is gaining strength by the moment.

"After the period of mourning, Jonathan's family began to worry about finding me another husband among their numbers. This I could not do, so I took refuge in the temple. Within months, my prayers and fasting and refusal to leave convinced them. They thought I was crazed with grief and they sought legal means to end their responsibility to me. We were all relieved."

"Oh, Anna, how could you do this?" Mary cries. "All these years and still grieving?" Her youthful love and optimism were appalled.

"You do not think I have grieved all these years? Sixty-three solid years of grief? That is what you think, child?" The young mother nods her head. She watches the floor instead of my face. Gently taking her face into my hands, I lift her countenance and looked deeply into her eyes. "Have you heard the Creator's voice?" I ask.

She does not hesitate. Her nod is certain and secure.

"Then you must know that those sixty-three years of listening were not centered on grief. Mary, child, you must know that. Grief forced me into prayer, but somewhere, in the rote prayers of our people, the Savior himself began to speak.

"That voice, Mary. You know the joy of that voice. You know the tenderness, the forgiveness, the awesome love in that voice. That voice is why I live, Mary. And now, today, you have let me see the one who will carry that voice through his earthly journey. Today I have held salvation himself in my arms. Think of it. Hearing his voice for sixty-three years and today I held that voice in my arms."

. . . .

PRAYER AS BREATHING

Prayer has always seemed a natural state for me. I do not know if this is because I began praying as a child, or if it is because I did not cease praying as I left childhood. Nancy Roth's image of prayer as the breath of God, the breath he breathed into us to form a living creature, has always attracted me. She states, "Prayer is the means whereby we let the Spirit of God breathe in and through us. . . . Prayer is not something we need to learn, as much as a remembering who we are. To live and breathe the breath of God is the reason we were created."

In Thessalonians we are exhorted to pray without ceasing. We breathe without ceasing; surely we should pray without ceasing. It makes perfect, symmetrical sense to me. But prayer is an elusive thing. It is a path not clearly marked, one that needs the intervention and sustaining guidance of mentors to keep us on it.

HEARING GOD'S VOICE IN PRAYER

When I was a child, the path of prayer seemed easy to follow. Why, as a young adult, did I need the lessons taught to me again, taught by a circle of sisters who knew the labyrinths of prayer deep in their souls?

I suppose it was because my childhood had been formed by good Baptist folk who gave us Bibles, told us that prayer was just talking to God and then sent us off to "hear God." That experience was both natural and profound. It was part of my spiritual formation. These early mentors had trusted the Holy Spirit in a child's heart.

By my teenage years, we were in a more sophisticated world theologically. It was a world that did not trust a child's heart to hear and communicate with the Almighty. I needed to set aside this dangerous, hearing form of prayer. My youth director said so.

I tried hard not to hear and to commit myself to more formal prayers and to seek God with a more reserved vocabulary. I tried to limit the manner in which he spoke.

By my senior year of college I was weary of such prayer. I wanted to converse with God. And God was faithful to send an old prayer warrior to teach me how to do so. Rosalind Rinker, author of *Prayer: Conversing with God,* came to my college the spring of my senior year and taught me to become a child again, to converse with God. She mentored me, although she never knew my name. Her impact has been profound.

The day was warm. We had gathered in a large room, where she was to teach fifty or sixty college students to pray. She grouped us into small sections of five or six individuals, then gave us instructions: we could pray one sentence, then we would need silence. We would need to listen. Only when we were certain where the Holy Spirit was leading would we go on to another sentence.

For Rosalind, prayer was to be conversational. If we did not silence ourselves, we could not hope to hear God's reply.

Breathless, we asked her how we would know God had replied. I remember her shaking her head with amusement. "Don't you know the Shepherd's voice? Goodness, what has kept you praying if he hasn't replied?"

Timidity struck us silent. She heard the voice of God. How could we admit that we were ignorant? I remembered that I always heard the voice of God as a child. But I had been warned off such "foolishness." Now, here was a grown woman, a clear window into the love of God, telling me she could hear.

"Children, you hear his voice in different ways. Maybe a verse of Scripture will come to mind. Maybe a hymn. Maybe someone else in the circle will pray, and that person's words will strike you as coming from him. Now get in your circles and converse with God."

Our circle nervously joined hands. Standing, we fidgeted until one of the Bible majors took over and began to pray. Three or four sentences into his brave prayer, a hand fell softly on his shoulder. "Son, one sentence and then listen. You must listen. You cannot go on until you or one of your group hears enough to know where to go on to." I studied the carpet patterns, grateful that I had not tried.

That gentle hand fell frequently throughout that day, admonishing in love, correcting with a squeeze and forcing all of us to embrace a different form of prayer—a prayer that seeks rapport with the Creator. Sociologists today would term it a very feminine style of prayer, an attempt to know God, to communicate with God and to have God communicate with us.

The afternoon was revolutionary. We fell in love with prayer. We fell in love with each other and were completely turned on by the power of group prayer. We prayed through lunch and into the next class. We had to be turned out of the room so that others could use it. That prayer, that hearing-the-voice-of-God prayer, had an intimacy and power that few of us had ever experienced.

I had never met anyone who so radiated the love, joy and acceptance of Jesus as Rosalind did. Every gesture, every smile, twinkled with the love of the Savior. Someday, when I too have walked with Jesus for sixty or seventy years, I hope I can radiate his love that way.

THE WAYS WE HEAR GOD

Years passed. I grew comfortable again with my childhood understanding of prayer. I called to mind a little girl who was confident in hearing. Therefore, it was no surprise to me that one of my daughters wanted to know how to hear God. My six-year-old, mischievous Rachael.

"How do you hear God, Mom?" she asked, fresh from the kindergarten classroom. "How do you know when it's him talking and not just you talking to yourself?" Six years old. She wants to know how to hear God and she is only six.

How do we hear God? Audibly? In the quiet of our hearts? In the mind's eye? How? At this point in my life, my daughter's question and my friends' and mentors' answers led me deeper in my understanding of prayer. I began to study the Word and wrote Rachael a short story about how different individuals she knows and loves hear God.

In John 10, Jesus calls himself the good shepherd, and we are his sheep. This is how he explains it:

The man who enters by the gate is the shepherd of his sheep. The watchman opens the gate for him, and the sheep listen to his voice. He calls his own sheep by name and leads them out. When he has brought out all his own, he goes on ahead of them, and his sheep follow him because they know his voice.

But they will never follow a stranger; in fact, they will run away from him because they do not recognize a stranger's voice. (John 10:2-5)

We are supposed to recognize the voice of God. Yet the ways we hear the voice of God are as varied as the forms of prayer. We come from different backgrounds and have learned different ways to pray. Some of us are most comfortable with memorized words. Others converse freely as beloved children. There is great value in both forms. Both routes will take us to the same destination: the throne of God. A woman in our church said it best: "Prayer is like watering a garden. There are many ways to get the water to the garden. I can carry it in a bucket, use a hose or wait for rain. Prayer is like that . . . from determined activity to grateful satisfaction."

Always, if it is the voice of God I am hearing, it lines up with the written Word of God. All of it. Sometimes if what I hear is the silence of God and the hopefulness of Carol, confusion reigns. And God is not a god of confusion.

When I feel the Spirit of God impressing something on my heart, speaking to me in his special way, I check the impression with Scripture. If it lines up with the Word of God, I begin to meditate on it. I say the words over and over and begin to ask questions of God. I share it with a small circle of trusted friends and mentors.

Several years ago, Dad had surgery. My dear friend Cathy, not knowing about the surgery, sent me a worship tape. On it were these words regarding heaven: ". . . when I finally put sight to the voice I've embraced." Those words brought instant tears to my eyes, and still do. The voice, God's voice—I have hungered after that voice since I was a child. I have found that voice in my own way, learning to identify it through trial and error. I have hurt others and myself by putting words into his mouth. I have eaten the bitter fruit of such mistakes and pressed on.

THE NECESSITY OF MENTORS IN PRAYER

Prayer is a spiritual discipline that requires mentoring. We need those who have spent much time on their knees to teach us the path. We need them to hear our reflections. We need them to carefully sift through our lives and assure us that what we believe God is saying actually lines up with the written Word of God.

This requires great vulnerability and humility. With an open heart, we need to ask our teachers and mentors to help us hear. Vulnerability and the hearing prayers of the believers are inseparable. Vulnerability keeps us honest in our mentoring circles. And it safeguards us from the humiliating and damaging experiences in prayer that many in the body of Christ suffer. We all have heard of those experiences. Often they begin with the words, "I have heard God say that you . . ." I do not know if God ever corrects individuals publicly. I find that the gentle, quiet voice of the Holy Spirit does its correction privately, moving us to repentance as opposed to public humiliation. I know that I greatly prefer the correction of my own soul to be done in private by a loving God.

My son, Noah, has mentored me in prayer, teaching me from when he was just a little guy. One night we were in the car, along with my daughter Rachael and friend Lori, who may have had a too-exalted view of our family. That evening Lori was treated to a "reality hit" with my children and me.

"Mom," says eight-year-old Rachael, commanding our attention. "Mom, I know you wrote me that cute story on how to hear God."

"Yes, Rachael," I say, concentrating on the country road I am negotiating. It had been two years since I'd written it.

"Mom!" The command is more strident. "Mom, I still don't get it. I don't think you have taught me all that well. I am not hearing God." Lori steals a glance at me. I smile, shaking my head.

"Rachael, honey, hearing God is a very long lesson. Remember in the story? You started with the first lesson that God is everywhere and so is his voice. Next we will teach you more about recognizing that voice." My voice is lecturing. I could be in class, a teacher with a rather obtuse student, not a sympathetic mom. I am also trying hard to let Lori know that it's not my fault this child doesn't understand.

"Mom," interrupts Noah, age six. "I don't hear God so good either. You know, I don't really hear him much at all. So, here's what I decided." Lori and I exchange grins in the darkness. "I talk to him, and when I can't hear him, I just . . ." The suspense builds; his breath is held in tight. "I just make up an answer for him!" His enthusiasm is felt in the rush of breath that escapes with his answer. "And Mom! Mostly I choose *yes!*" he finishes triumphantly.

Lori and I laugh all the way to the garage. We laugh at the honesty of a child. We laugh with genuine love and appreciation for the children who are so good at teaching their moms lessons.

What Noah said is often true of all God's children. We don't hear so good. Sometimes we make up an answer for him. Mostly we say yes. And while the error of this method is brutally and hilariously apparent, so is the love of God for his son, Noah, and all his children.

We weren't angry with Noah. We explained why we mustn't put words into God's mouth. We loved on him and giggled with him and corrected him in an air of joy. All of this was possible because six-year-olds are too wise to guard against vulnerability. As adults, we live in constant guardedness against exposing our true selves. Children seem to be on good terms with vulnerability; they seem to understand that there is no condemnation for a learning child.

Hearing God is a lesson we begin at birth and will only perfect when we finally see him face to face, when we finally put sight to the voice we've embraced. Imagine that. Imagine hearing his voice and finally seeing his face. Tracing his features with your very own hands. Stumbling in awe, overwhelmed by love and being reassured by the voice you have followed so long.

Kneeling in Private

Jesus tells us to approach God privately, in a place unseen by men. He is recommending a place where we can communicate freely without the need to put on airs. God has reasons for these instructions. His reasons protect us; they keep us from making fools of ourselves. His reasons involve seeing ourselves as the children of God that we are—heirs of eternity, joint heirs of Christ—yet children. Little, squirmy, difficult-to-teach children.

Diane is one of my favorite people on planet earth. She is a transplant from Arkansas, having lived in the Pacific Northwest for thirty years or so. But still, at the heart of it all, she is a storytelling Southerner. She has been a wonderful mentor in several areas of life, none more so than in prayer.

Diane tells a wonderful story about being a child in prayer. She understands what it means to take long months to meditate on a truth, in prayer, until the answer becomes apparent. It is a story we all love. We love it because we know Diane to be a mature, trustworthy woman of prayer, a woman whose walk with God is admired by all of us close enough to watch.

Here is that story: Diane had a dear friend who had chosen badly. This woman was living for the moment. She had walked away from Jesus to satisfy her own desires. Diane grieved over this woman's decision like she had never grieved before. She stormed the throne of God and begged for this woman to turn from her sin. She pleaded, cajoled, bargained. You name it, Diane tried it. The woman stayed rooted in her sin.

Finally the Holy Spirit gave Diane a prayer—a profound prayer.

She prayed it daily for month upon month. It went like this: "Lord, I pray that you will strengthen her legs. Make her strong enough to kneel before you in repentance."

On and on Diane prayed, saying the words over and over again. "Strengthen her legs. Make her strong enough to kneel." She shared her prayer with us. She travailed in prayer.

Then one morning, six months or more into this daily—sometimes hourly—discipline of prayer, the Savior himself came and gently touched this little woman from Arkansas. "Diane," he said, "you have the prayer wrong. The prayer is not for your friend. It is for you!"

The blinders fell off. Focused on her friend's sin, she had not seen her own. Her own repentance was behind schedule. Her legs were the ones that needed strengthening. She needed to kneel.

Isn't that true of all of us? Is there a single child of God alive today who does not have her own weedy garden to tend? We look at each other and are quick to point, quick to offer help, quick to judge.

Jesus, our strong and ever-patient Savior, stands in the gardens of our lives, gently tugging our attention back. Jesus shows us the patches that need to be uprooted. It is Jesus who suggests that we try knee bends and graciously recommends that we do so in private. We are not public spectacles but protected children, learning the lessons of kneeling with the only One kind enough to teach us our prayers of repentance in private.

Diane got up from her knees. The work was done. She would never forget the lesson. And instead of feeling discouraged, she felt lighthearted. She was laughing about it, sharing it with her own circle of friends and mentors. Diane was fully convinced that he who revealed her sin to her had forgiven it and was laughing too. Not long after Diane got the lesson in knee bends, her friend found repentance, no doubt encouraged by the repentance of others.

LITURGICAL PRAYER

In the crucibles of life, we often are certain we have heard incorrectly. The pain is too great, the road too long. Yet we are drawn back to Paul's letter to the church in Thessolanica. "Pray continually." Keep on, even in prison. Continue until the last dying breath. Work until the painting is finished, the manuscript typed, the baby born. Keep on until that mission we were created to fulfill has been accomplished in its entirety.

Shortly after my mother's death, the lessons of keeping on became important to me. I found prayer to be difficult, knowing that my God had chosen to take Mom home at an early age. I knew he could have changed things and given me a longer time with Mom. Prayer became work, and I needed help. I longed to have the tenacity of Anna. I wanted to be able to pray long hours, to be devoted to prayer. Like Anna, my heart had been crushed by grief, and I needed to find a way to speak to God through tears.

Help came from a constant source, from my circle of sisters. It has been a blessing in this life to have a wide and varied circle of sisters, sisters from the strictest fundamentalist circles, sisters from the most liberal of circles, Catholic sisters, charismatic sisters, Baptist sisters, Episcopalian sisters, nondenominational sisters. All with a keen love of Jesus Christ. All dedicated to the conversion of their own souls into his image. All anticipating that moment when we see him face to face, when we finally put sight to the voice we've embraced. All mentoring me and allowing me to mentor them. All working toward the same goal.

Two of these sisters are about three years into a project: teaching me, ever so slowly, about the joys of liturgical prayer. Michelle is a stay-at-home mom who homeschools her daughter and runs the church soup kitchen. Anne has grown children, lives alone and is the head librarian in town. Both are tenderly and tenaciously committed to Jesus.

Feeling foolish, I ask them about liturgical prayer, their treasured form. Anne, ever the scholar, says it is "a pattern of language and prayer established by the ancient church. A prescribed method of prayer." I take notes dutifully, then look up for a simpler explanation.

Seeing my confusion, Anne laughs and says, "Carol, the Lord's Prayer is liturgical prayer, the Psalms are liturgical prayer. You'll find them throughout the *Book of Common Prayer*. Think of it as praying Scripture back to God."

I have long loved the discipline of praying Scripture back to God. It seems to inform my spirit better than almost any other form of prayer. Praying Scripture is a very safe and profound form of prayer. It instructs our hearts and minds and also lines up our wills with the will of God. Praying Scripture mentors my heart and my mind and my will.

But the *Book of Common Prayer* was another thing. "I've never really understood it," I admit. "I get lost in it. How can all that wordiness become a satisfying prayer?"

"Carol, it is a focused meditation," Michelle says. "Once you know the words, the pattern, then the language becomes a part of you. It is good theology set in beautiful prose. Once you know the words, you move past them into worship."

Then I ask these two my favorite question: "What does 'praying in the Spirit' mean to you?" I have asked that question to many people over the years. The answers are always thought provoking. Michelle's answer is no exception: "When I do not know how to pray, the memorized prayers of the church come to me, instructing my prayer. I feel a great connection to the cloud of witnesses mentioned in Hebrews. Here I am, part of a huge family of God, a family that has used these same words for centuries. A family whose creed has not changed."

I ask for their favorite prayers from the *Book of Common Prayer*. And because I am a writer, a woman whose work is with words, I am charmed, fed deeply in my soul, by their replies. "At night I like one prayer because it covers all the bases," Michelle says. "Keep watch, dear Lord, with those who work, or watch, or weep this night, and give your angels charge over those who sleep. Tend the sick, Lord Christ; give rest to the weary, bless the dying, soothe the suffering, pity the afflicted, shield the joyous; and all for your love's sake. Amen."

"Yes, that is a good one," Anne says. "But what about the evening prayer? The one whose language is poetry?" The two women grin, and then Anne prays: "O Lord, support us all the day long, until the shadows lengthen, and the evening comes, and the busy world is hushed, and the fever of life is over, and our work is done. Then in thy mercy, grant us a safe lodging, and a holy rest and peace at the last. Amen."

Poetry and prayer. I understand the validity of the form. There is great power in repetition and the worship that occurs once words are learned and the meaning sets into our bones. Using the prayers of God's people, the rote, memorized language of poetry, allowed me to worship during that time of mourning, to line up my heart with the heart of God. It gave me a path back into prayer.

When God Is Silent

There are times when prayer is anything but poetry, times when it is agonizing and feels barren. There are seasons when it seems we are storming a heaven devoid of habitation.

The lesson from these seasons of silence, these times when prayer seems an exercise in futility, is to persevere. Hannah storms heaven's gates for a period, and finally God opens her womb. Elizabeth is an old woman when her prayers are answered as she had hoped. David's prayers do not save his kingdom, but the Savior comes from his lineage. Job continues to pray when all of life is taken from him, and the result is a clearer view of God and a restoration of blessing in this life. Anna's years of prayers culminate in holding salvation himself in her arms. There are women in my circle who have prayed for children, husbands, parents for years. While God has remained silent, they have trusted the heart of their Savior.

Praying when God is silent is an act of faith. It is belief in God's ultimate goodness in the absence of visible proof. It is believing that God will weave all of our experiences into good, when all we see are the very dark lines of a current trial. Such prayer is highly honored by God. It must be honored by those of us privileged enough to participate also.

JESUS, OUR MENTOR IN PRAYER

When we speak of a life of prayer, it seems to me that Jesus remains the perfect mentoring example. At times he prayed the liturgical prayers of his people. At times he spoke spontaneously to God. At times he reported. In all, he had an ever deeper rapport with the Father.

Many times in Jesus' ministry he prayed and healed. The work was done instantaneously. Then Scripture tells us an amazing thing: As the interest of the crowds grew, Jesus, who could have just kept on conquering illness and disease, went off alone to commune with God. You see, as important as it was that he conquer sin and death, it was equally important that he maintain a relationship with the Father.

Luke 4 tells us of Jesus' visit to the home of Simon, where he healed Simon's mother-in-law. Word spread quickly and Jesus spent the evening healing everyone in the area. In the morning, just when the second wave of truly needy people was waking up to the wonderful news of a healer, Jesus went to a solitary place. Scripture tells us that people were looking everywhere for him. Imagine the intensity of their search. Imagine his host family trying to explain his absence. After all, what could possibly be more important than healing the sick?

Where was he? Conversing with his Father. Ministry did not take him away from that sacred conversation. Luke tells us, "The news about him spread all the more, so that crowds of people came to hear him and to be healed of their sicknesses. But Jesus *often* withdrew to lonely places and prayed" (5:15-16, emphasis added).

To me this is a difficult lesson. When people are needy, when they beg for help, it is very difficult to say, "You just don't understand. I need to retreat to a lonely place and converse with God." Guilt and shame taunt me. Yet the example set by Jesus is solid. It occurs in every Gospel. He seeks the Father, regardless of the crowds, of the needy people around him and of the political points he fails to score when he leaves.

I am told to be like him. To discern those times when I am to walk through the crowd and off to the lonely place. No, the public does not clamor to see me, but my children do. And there are times when my children watch Disney in the family room while Mom is holed up in her bedroom, door locked, alone with Jesus. There are times when the church needs another set of capable hands, and mine are clasped in prayer.

The new president of Yale University said it best. He said that the busyness of his job scared him. He said that if he did not have the time to put his feet up on the desk, gaze out the window and dream, then he might manage Yale University but he would never lead it. What a profound truth! We might manage, but we'll never lead a hurting world back to Jesus—not even if we are caught up in a multitude of good works, because nothing can take the place of that time of meditative prayer.

Today Rachael is begging for more lessons on prayer. Snuggled deep in the armchair, my little one and I begin the journey. Knowing that her heart so desires him, we take his example and begin:

Our Father, who art in heaven,
Hallowed be Thy name.
Thy kingdom come,
Thy will be done,
On earth as it is in heaven.
Give us this day
Our daily bread.
And forgive us our debts,
As we forgive our debtors.
Lead us not into temptation,
But deliver us from evil.
For Thine is the kingdom,
And the power, and the glory,
Forever. Amen. (See Matthew 6:9-13.)

Over time we will use his words and our words. We will come in joy and in anguish. We will come for comfort as well as sustenance. We will breathe in the cleansing breath of God, and prayer will expel from our lives the damaging vestiges of the enemy's schemes. We will learn more about solitary prayer, more about the sacred silences of God. We will strive to be comfortable when he is silent, knowing that it is all covered, all secure in his nail-torn hands.

And while we will never perfect the art of hearing, one day, when we see him face to face, "it will be worth all the waiting . . . for that one moment of celebrating!"

FOR REFLECTION AND DISCUSSION

1. Who has a prayer life you envy? Why is her prayer life so powerful? Can you ask her? What do you love about prayer?

2. Prayer is communicating. It is remembering who we are, who created us and then forging a constant and direct line of communica-

tion with our Creator. Read the following verses and think about when you are to pray. How do these verses change the way you live today?

- 1 Thessalonians 5:17
- 2 Thessalonians 1:11
- Acts 1:14

3. What guidelines does Scripture give us for how we are to pray? Let these Scriptures get your study started.

- Matthew 6:5-13
- Luke 6:28
- 1 Peter 4:7

Who Am I?

. . . .

So God created man in his own image, in the image of God he cre-
ated him; male and female he created them. . . . When God cre-
ated man, he made him in the likeness of God. He created them
male and female and blessed them. And when they were created,
he called them "man."

GENESIS 1:27; 5:1-2

EVE'S STORY

Grandma? What was it like in the Garden?"

My granddaughter's question halts all conversation around the fire. My daughters and the older granddaughters know. I do not speak of the Garden. The Garden remains such a painful memory that I do not revisit it, even in my dreams.

Rasa tells her daughter to be quiet. Devorah's dark curls hide cheeks that are crimson with embarrassment. This is her first time in the circle of women. She is just twelve, just old enough to join the women at the firelight.

Devorah is one of my favorites. She reminds me of Cain. Impulsive, eager to please, always caught doing the wrong thing. And like any grandmother who has lost a child, I am only too anxious to indulge his likeness.

"Leave her, Rasa. Perhaps it is time. Perhaps you should know about the Garden from my eyes. Perhaps . . ." My mind wanders off as it does often these days. The Garden, guarded now by cherubim with a flaming sword, remains my highest hope and my deepest regret.

"Grandma?" Devorah prompts, reminding me of her presence. All these women around the fire, all my seed, all wanting to know. Love now prompts the exposure of my shame. It is right that they know.

"The Garden. That is what you want to know?" I ask. Heads bob in agreement. My audience is eager; only the storyteller is reluctant.

"Well, Devorah, the Garden was a paradise. There the animals lived together in harmony. Your grandfather Adam named them and together we learned their ways and their habits. They lived in harmony also. I named the plants, and after careful observation, Adam and I learned their habits as well.

"And every evening . . . ah, the evening . . . that was when God came. God walked with us, side by side in the Garden, just as the night air cooled the land. And we lived in harmony with God."

"Grandma?" asks Jana's second child. "What does God look like?"

I pause, wondering how to explain glory to human eyes . . . eyes that know only the fallen world. "God looks like . . . child, God is like the wind. Only God's wind is covered in flame and sound and light and . . . and glory. Child, God is glory."

"I do not know what glory is like," Jana admits. No, I don't suppose any of them know what glory is like. Not in this God-forsaken world.

"Mama?" she says. "If the animals were in harmony, and the plants were in harmony, were you and father in harmony too?"

Laughter fills the air. Jana married Seth and finds life with him hard. It is difficult to live with someone who is always right. But Seth is my son. If he is always right about everything, perhaps it is because his parents were so very wrong. Perhaps he too is forever tainted by our sin. I reply, "Yes, Jana. In the Garden Adam and I were in complete harmony."

"How was that? How did you keep that?" she asks, ignoring the chuckles of her sisters.

"It was a different world. You see, Adam and I were created to reflect the image of God. We were created to be like him. So Adam reflected some areas of God, and some areas we both reflected, and some areas I reflected alone. So you see, we were equal. You needed both of us to see the entire image God had given the world of himself. Seeing just one of us was like seeing half a picture."

This explanation causes much whispering. I am sorrowful. In my shame, I have not schooled my daughters in the glory they reflect. I have failed to pass on to them their own unique mission, their calling. Somehow they do not know that they also reflect a side of God.

"But, Mama, if this is so," begins Rasa, nervous about the path her thoughts are following, "if this is true, why does father rule over you?" I am an old woman. My hands shake constantly without the pressure of this exposure. Now my sin must be revealed. Confessed.

"Does it all go back to your mistake with the fruit?" Devorah asks.

"Yes, little one. It all goes back to that," I admit, grateful that she has made my way an easier one. "Before we ate that fruit, your grandfather and I delighted in our differences. We delighted in each other. We were partners in everything. Everything we did together."

The contrast is painful for me to remember. The soul mate of the Garden has long since given way to a man who watches me with long, bitter silences. I have found it easier to be angry with Adam, to be hurt and to cling to that hurt, than to examine the truth behind the hurt. I continue: "You see, when the serpent tempted me, your grandfather was standing right next to me. He did not stop me; in fact, when I offered it to him, his hand was extended.

"When God asked Adam what had happened, Adam blamed it on me.

"I think your grandfather has always been a little ashamed of his words that day. He and I know the truth of the story. And God knew the truth too. Just as we had partnered in everything else, Adam had partnered with me in taking the fruit.

"Then, when we were forced out of the Garden, Adam was angry with me and with himself, and we were both sick with shame. It never left us. We wore the skins of the white bears we had loved so much. Their sacrifice would forever taint us. And I was terribly ashamed; I had led us into disaster."

"But, Mama, Daddy had taken it too. He was also guilty," cried Rasa.

"Yes, your father is also guilty." I sigh. "But I still love your father. I do not have it in me to expose him to himself. If it is easier to blame me . . ." my shaking hands express my inability to continue.

The fireside is quiet. The flames of firelight leap toward the sky. I recall a young Adam, leaping with the deer, running races with antelope. I recall a perfect union that we have never achieved this side of Eden.

My throat closes. I can explain no more to this circle. Our eyes move as one to the flash of the cherubim's sword. The Garden is closed.

. . . .

CREATED FEMALE IN GOD'S IMAGE?

Circles of women. Ageless circles. Women gathering around the firelight, around the kitchen table, around the garden stoop, all wanting to know, all wanting to discover what it means to be female. To be created in the very image of God, and be female. To have been fashioned from that area of God that is relational to the core, that desires intimacy, that uses lots and lots of language.

Growing up in a small Baptist church, I often felt somewhat left out of the community of faith that spanned the centuries. After all, everyone knows about David and Joshua, about Abraham and Noah.

But what about the little girls of Scripture? What about the heroines of faith? Were there any stories about them?

In fairness, my small church did what they could, way back then, to teach us the stories of Esther and Sarah, of Elizabeth and Lydia. They acknowledged that there were women of merit throughout the holy book. But what seemed to be missing was a deep understanding of woman as created in the image of God, a belief that all that is woman is somehow found in the person of God.

This is a difficult and abstract concept. God cannot be dissected based on gender, because God encompasses both genders. We can study pronouns and agree that female pronouns are used in Scripture to refer to God, especially relating to the Holy Spirit. At the same time, there is no desire on anyone's part to negate the maleness that Christ inhabited as the Messiah. No one would try to deny the wonderful and affirming passages of Scripture that refer to God as Father. So where does that leave woman? This was my frequent question in my twenties and early thirties.

Two mentors worked in tandem to help me unravel this puzzle. Miss Cambridge was my Bible teacher at college. A single woman with a passion for books, she fed my spirit on a deep and permanent level. She could give more information in a forty-five-minute lecture than anyone I have encountered. Brilliant.

Miss Cambridge was the first woman to teach me that all that is female and all that is male are found in the person of God. God holds the paradox of male and female in his very person and is complete, whole and holy. God is all that is male and all that is female.

"In the image of God he created him; male and female he created them" (Genesis 1:27). Scripture gives us no room to look for an outward source of inspiration when it came to creation. The creation of woman was done by patterning her after God. Anything less is heresy. But less is often what we've settled for. Less than the image of God.

Less than that element of God that we were patterned after. Failing to celebrate the image we were created from, we have instead settled for a broken image, one that fails to acknowledge the greatness woman was patterned after.

Miss Cambridge reminded me that I am created to reflect the God of the universe—the relational, intimate God of the universe. Then Ernestine came along a few years later. She became my mentor when I had the information solidly in my head and in my heart and needed to learn how to put it into my life. She was honest about the conflict I was bound to feel inside church walls. Having equality in my profession would not translate into the church easily. The concept of honoring a woman's thoughts and ideas as equal to those of her brothers is one the church continues to struggle with. Ernestine taught me how to live with a work in process.

WHAT DOES IT MEAN TO BE FEMALE?

I was a child of the sixties and seventies. In school I was taught to believe that anything men can do, I'd better learn to do better. My generation was going to change things. We would do and have it all: the best careers, the best marriages, the best kids.

I grew up with a sister and no brothers, and I gave birth to two girls. I thought I had it down. Then my son was born. As different from my girls as night is from day. Every bit as wonderful. Every bit as loved. But different. Male.

The girls were talking at one year. They loved to talk. They still love to talk. We three can talk all day and then talk all night. My son uses words when he needs to. And he began his linguistic discoveries by making sounds like "vroom vroom" and "bang bang." He uses language to report to me, to give me the facts of the day, just like his dad does. The girls give me all of the day's ambiance. They flood my ears with stories and word pictures and textures of conversations.

Yes, boys and girls are different. I wasn't expecting that. I was a product of my time, expecting that, "raised correctly," there would be few notable differences. Wrong! There are hundreds of differences. Thousands. And the differences are wonderful. They are things to rejoice in. These differences broaden and expand our understanding. They are a gift to us.

Psychologists tell us this is so. While these are categories that do not fit all men or all women, the generalizations hold true for the majority. They tell us that from the time a girl is born, she is actively pursuing intimacy. Boys are driven toward independence. She learns language quicker than her brothers, because she wants to relate. He learns to manipulate objects through space. (Remember bows and arrows? Or video games? All products of the male mind.)

She uses thousands more words every day than he does. She develops best friends and works with diligence to keep those friends. He works to understand games and how to win. Hierarchy is essential to him.

By adolescence, the signs of a broken world set in. In this broken world, she is willing to give up her natural giftings in the realms of literature, science, music and math to concentrate solely on having a "good body" because she wants boys to notice and give her the spiritual and psychological intimacy she craves. In this broken world, he sees women as a thing to be conquered, a sign of his success. He will bankrupt his relationships to serve a need to be the best.

To a woman, relationships have an incredibly high priority at the core of who she is. And because she lives in a broken world, her giftings are often ignored or belittled. Relationships are fleeting and her need for them can be degrading. She is taught to compete with her sisters instead of complement them. Her body is seen as a tool to obtain intimacy, and the brokenness is passed on to future generations. Her need for spiritual intimacy is often silenced, and she is told that her experience is not worthy of the church's consideration.

For a man, conquering has an incredibly high priority at the core of who he is. He is driven to be the best, to climb higher and run faster. And because he lives in a broken world, his giftings are often denigrated or passed off as politically incorrect. He is taught to compete with his brothers instead of building a strong community with them. His need for spiritual intimacy is often seen as softness, and he is taught to hide it.

But this is not what was planned. Her giftings were to be honored, celebrated, rejoiced in and used. This broken self-image is not what she was created to be. This is all a mixed-up, fixed-up counterfeit. Neither is it what was planned for men. His gifting were to be used and celebrated. He was not designed to be emotionally silent or spiritually absent. It is all a mixed-up, fixed-up counterfeit.

So what was the original? Glory!

The original was unbroken. Her drive for relational intimacy was unsoiled with counterfeits. Her need for linguistic repartee was rejoiced in. She was proud of the aspects of God she reflected, confident in her calling, able to walk with God in the cool of the evening, face to face, unspoiled. The same was true for men.

CELEBRATING THE IMAGE OF GOD IN WOMEN

I often find myself thinking about that original plan and wondering if there is a way back. Have you ever wondered what it would be like to live every day with a consciousness of the image we reflect? Have you wondered how that would change our world? Just as I was beginning to ask this question I was blessed to take a class, "The Image of God in Man," taught by Christian counselor Dr. Larry Day. Larry tells a wonderful story about taking his son to see the Olympic torch as it passed through Portland. He talked about the honor it was just to see it pass by. He talked about the joy and excitement on the faces of those who were allowed the privilege of carrying it. And he watched his son's eyes grow larger with each passing moment.

At home that night, Larry sat alone and wondered. What would it be like if those of us who are privileged to bear the image of God in our very souls carried that image with the awe and respect that those runners carried the Olympic torch? Image bearers of the Creator of the universe—what would it be like?

I have thought about the women in my life who have celebrated that identity. I have thought about Miss Cambridge and how she worshiped God with her mind. In an era when the majority of women married and had families, she was an unusual woman, devoting herself to God and the study of theology. She liked being a woman and she liked being a scholar.

My friend Wendy is an artist. She is all woman, female to her core. She is also creative to her core. Wendy loves Jesus and has worked hard to accept that, while she is different from most of her sisters, she is loved by God. She is created in his very image, and the creative streak that dominates her draws the rest of us closer to the Creator.

Mark's mom is relational to her core. Her family and friends are her life and have been for eighty-some years now. She delights in them. She continues to show up at a friend's door with a custard, to quilt a comforter for a grandchild, to keep her circle surrounded with her love. She reflects back the caring, relational heart of God, and we are all warmed by it.

All of these women reflect back the image they were created in. All of them celebrate their Creator. They mentor and teach and coach us as we look to their faces to find the face we long for: the face of God.

MODELING THAT IDENTITY

Modeling that identity is important for all of us. We need to find those we can learn from and then model that identity for women who need to see our spin on the original. We need mentors faithful to what God created them to be.

We also need to recognize that each step of our journey is useful to someone. I think about the circle of women I know and their gifts at each stage of life. Maria reminds us how important it is to genuinely love our spouse. She is a lovely young woman and the devoted mother of three young boys. I enjoy watching her with her children, but I love watching her with her husband, Brian. Her face comes alive when he enters a room. All is right with her world when Brian is at home. I know they have conflicts like any couple, but I also know that her love for him is a solid foundation that anyone can learn from.

Anne is the mother of two very active little boys. She adores them and they adore their mommy. She reminds me regularly of the unconditional love we are given for our children and the love God holds for us. Dave and Anne have given their boys a rock-solid foundation with their love for each other and their lively, exuberant, unconditional love for them.

Lisa is a businesswoman whose last child went to college this year. She runs the photography business that she owns with her husband. Good with clients—soothing those high school seniors who come for that all-important senior photo—she is incredible with hospitality. Lisa is the hostess for Apples of Gold at our church, and she makes *every* woman feel welcome. She reminds me of the graciousness God gives us. She is the definition of *graciousness*.

Penny is my model for retirement. She was a bank executive until she retired a couple of years ago. Since then she has remained actively involved in our church and has used her gifts to work on our building campaign, mentor our women, mentor our leaders and spread as much love and understanding around as possible. She is a reminder for me that my vocational involvement may end, but my place in the kingdom will remain ongoing and needed. Penny is a servant who has continued to serve.

Each of these women has reflected back to me the image they were created in. They have been windows into the person of God. They are standard bearers, torch holders, Olympians in life.

BROKEN IMAGES REFLECT HEALING

None of us is whole. None of us has reached adulthood without broken places in our lives. We live in a fallen world, and all of us yearn for the wholeness we were created to reflect.

It is a gift of enormous measure to share our brokenness with others. Sharing allows others to see areas in which God is at work. It allows them into the Healer's office to watch the miracle begin. And it reassures us that the miracle we seek can be found at his feet.

I know many women who have opened up their brokenness for others to see. They are courageous women who have allowed us to see the formidable brokenness caused by domestic violence, sexual abuse, bankruptcy, infidelity, eating disorders and a host of other attacks on the soul.

I think particularly of a woman who lived through domestic abuse. She now serves a community of women who have been through the same kind of violence. Her honest sharing of her brokenness has allowed many other women to break free from the cycle.

She is one of the many women who are reflecting back the image of God to a hurting world. They are allowing others to see how the Healer heals. I am honored to call them sisters because they are truly doing the work of the gospel. They are reflecting God's image of wholeness into a broken world. They are proclaiming the good news of a God who loves them, who wants to bring wholeness into their lives. They are the evangelists I admire most.

BACK TO THE GARDEN

I know the reality of brokenness; what I hunger for is wholeness. I want to find the original, to know if there is a way back to the Garden. Is there a way back to that time prior to the Fall, when Adam and Eve lived in perfect community with God? Adam and Eve did, you know. They reflected glory—God's glory. They lived in harmony with one another, and as a result of that harmony, the reflection of all that God is, they were taking dominion over the earth.

Imagine for a moment that harmony. Imagine male and female in perfect understanding, in perfect honor, working together in wholeness and community. In our broken world, it is often hard to begin to picture this. The abuses on both sides are too strong. The rhetoric is too loud. The picture, if it can be obtained at all, is too fuzzy.

But not in the heart, mind and very person of God. God is the image from which we were created. And in God, there is perfect union, perfect harmony. We can reflect that. We are called to reflect that. Born with the image of God imprinted on our souls, our highest calling hearkens back to the Creator—to reflect his glory, to live in communion with God, to walk in the cool of the evening in his presence.

FOR REFLECTION AND DISCUSSION

1. Read Genesis 1:26-31 and Genesis 2:20-25. What was God's purpose in creating woman? What did God pattern woman after? What was the relationship between man and woman prior to the Fall?

2. Read Genesis 3. What are the results of the Fall for men and for women? How do you see that played out in your own life?

3. What do you like best about being a woman?

4. Who do you know that seems to be comfortable with her identity? What is it you admire about her?

Do I Really Need to Learn Confession?

· ·

So after Abram had been living in Canaan ten years, Sarai his wife took her Egyptian maidservant Hagar and gave her to her husband to be his wife. He slept with Hagar, and she conceived.

When she knew she was pregnant, she began to despise her mistress. Then Sarai said to Abram, "You are responsible for the wrong I am suffering. I put my servant in your arms, and now that she knows she is pregnant, she despises me. May the LORD judge between you and me."

"Your servant is in your hands," Abram said. "Do with her whatever you think best." Then Sarai mistreated Hagar; so she fled from her.

GENESIS 16:3-6

SARAI'S STORY

Dear God, I come to you to confess my wrong. Abram says we must admit our wrongdoing, so here I am.

I beat her, God. I took a broom handle and beat her until the other servants pulled me away. The anger was white hot. I have never been angry like that in my life. I couldn't even think, God. I just swung away at her. I wanted to kill her.

So I confess it: I beat her. But God, what good does confession do? I am not sorry. I would do it again; I may do it again. What good is this confession without any real repentance attached?

She slept with my husband and then bore him a son. I thought I would get a family from her. I was prepared to share my life, a little bit anyway. Instead I created a monster. She laughs at my barrenness. She mocks me with her chubby little brat. Last night she taunted me, baring her firm, brown breast. She said that Abram . . . she said. . . she wanted me to know that he . . .

Oh God, how could he do this thing? Why did he do this thing? I could kill her. I hate him.

This is useless. My confession is an empty one. I want my own child. I do not want that woman's child. I want that woman dead. God, can you change me? Can you take this mess that I've created and bring wholeness? Must I live with hatred for the rest of my life?

. . . .

What Is Confession?

Confession: an honest examination of one's sin. A time of exposure and forgiveness, experiencing the mysteries of salvation. Confession is not an easy topic and has not been a popular one in my lifetime. Nor, if I am honest, have I been eager to learn about confession, either as a child or as an adult. But confession is a discipline my mentors have been careful to teach me and to encourage as a daily practice.

Confession is not complete without repentance. Scripture does not tell us if Sarai ever confessed or repented of her treatment of Hagar. It was a situation steeped in emotion and frustration. Confession would have been her starting point, the place where she would have acknowledged the wrong she had done. Once we acknowledge a wrong, the Holy Spirit is able to begin the process that moves us from an admission of guilt to a commitment to never repeat the wrong.

While the subject of confession is a difficult one, it is a transforming concept, a concept learned best from friends and sisters. You may even call them mentors if you'd like!

PERSONAL CONFESSION

As my own children were born, I began to learn the most painful lesson of confession. It horrified me when my children began to mirror my own deeply private sin. There, blazing from the mouth of a four-year-old, my sin was reproduced. My unkind remarks, my driving frustrations, all the items that I moaned and groaned over with wickedly cruel remarks were reproduced in the voices of my children. In living color. And because we have three children, my sin was in surround sound.

During this time, I began to ask the Lord to teach me about confession. I learned that the word *confession* means to acknowledge one's guilt. I was at a point in life where acknowledging my guilt was no longer an option—it was an imperative. My guilt was running around being parroted by three very vocal, visible children.

John wrote, "If we confess our sins, he is faithful and just and will forgive us our sins and purify us from all unrighteousness" (1 John 1:9). This was exactly what my heart desired. I wanted to be free of sin and guilt. I wanted a thorough cleansing.

The frustration for me lay in the fact that I wanted confession to be a one-time thing, but I was beginning to suspect that sin and confession were never-ending. And once I began to institute a daily time to confess, it only got worse. Sins I never knew I had came up to introduce themselves. Again Jesus sent friends to help, those courageous sisters who live with daily times of confession in their own lives.

It is the Fourth of July. Wendy and I walk through her orchard, alone. All around the orchard are friends and family. The kids are playing and nagging their fathers for fireworks. Picnic tables hold the remains of a large midday meal. Women, done with the preparations and serving of that meal, sit in small circles, faces lifted to the sun, eyes closed, relaxing at last. Bees drone lazily, trying to find an uncovered dish.

"Wendy, I'm having the worst time spiritually," I begin, knowing that Wendy is a safe person for me to share my struggles with.

"What's wrong?" she asks.

"It's just that I'm spending all my time confessing. It never ends!" I exclaim, frustrated and embarrassed.

Her smile is wide, lips closed to keep the laughter from escaping. "Confession is a good thing," she replies.

"Yes, but all day long? Every day? I mean, my sin is *ever* before me. *Ever, ever, ever!*" I shout to the cathedral of trees.

"I'm sorry," she chuckles. "You're in a good place—it's okay. Did you think you weren't human? Did you think your sinful nature quit trying at salvation?" Her chuckles are not subdued. I wasn't chuckling.

"Yeah, but . . . I mean, before I started all this, I didn't feel all that guilty about much of anything. In fact, before the kids started mirroring my sin, I thought I was more or less all right."

I am forever grateful that my sisters keep teaching me, that so far no one has tarred and feathered me and shipped me out of town for arrogance. They are so gentle in spirit, they don't even laugh too often. Not usually, anyway.

"Carol," Wendy says, with voice kind but now serious and firm. "Do you want to be like Jesus?"

"Yes," I answer, certain.

"Then you must plan on a daily period of confession for the rest of your life."

"Seriously?" I ask, unbelieving.

"Seriously. To do anything less is spiritual arrogance and pride. Accept that in the realm of the spirit, we are all children. Children need to learn; they make mistakes. Children need to confess those mistakes to remain in a close relationship with the Father."

"Continual huh?" I ask.

"Continual like a house that never stays clean," she chuckles. "Carol, confession is not the same as conversation. It requires a knowledge of self and an ability to face one's flesh without flinching. It is a formal act done with seriousness and fear and trembling.

"If we don't acknowledge our continued need for confession, it is impossible to realize our desperate need for a savior. If we say we are 'clean before God,' we lie, because all have sinned and fallen short of the glory of God. Everyone has secret rooms—goodness, I have discovered whole floors in my soul. Those secret places are guarded against discovery at all costs. Because Jesus' great desire is wholeness for us, he wants us to voluntarily open those hidden rooms and let him clean them with us.

"And sometimes the cleaning requires that we make penance. Penance allows the sinner to contribute to the restitution of the wronged and to take responsibility for her own healing and restoration.

"That, my friend, is what confession is. It tells the truth, and it sets us free."

I am reminded of a wonderful quote from the first century, and I tell Wendy: "Confession of our faults is the next thing to innocence."

"That is wonderful," she sighs. "Innocence. If we want to walk in true innocence before the Father, we need to live in constant confession. Forever."

I walked out of the orchard, back into the picnic, feeling silent to my bones. In 1 Corinthians 4:4 the apostle Paul wrote, "My conscience is clear, but that does not make me innocent." This helps me to understand. Even Paul could not count on a pure heart. Wendy was right: I had to realize that I had not arrived. I would need to have a daily period of confession. I would never be able to neglect this new and difficult discipline again.

WHEN CONFESSION IS PUBLIC

This summer my high school class will begin to think about another reunion. In three years, we will celebrate thirty years since graduation. Amazing. Suddenly we have been out of high school for twenty-seven years.

One of the most profound lessons of my life began the fall of my senior year. I recall it with great emotion. Today I can see the scenes as vividly as during the days I lived them.

My senior year, I was fortunate. In a school with a first-rate music program, I was in the three top performing groups. Though never a soloist, I was a steady, dependable alto. My closest friends filled those three choirs. Anne and Joan sang soprano. Stacey was one of the strongest altos God ever invented. Brad was my mischievous partner in Swing Choir. We were coached, taught and mentored by one of the finest teachers I have ever had the privilege of knowing: Mr. B. Fred Hammack.

Joan was a cheerleader that fall, the first year we won the city championship in football. She also sang in the three top groups. Her senior year looked like everyone's dream come true. It was a golden era filled with wonderful friends, steady boyfriends and an amazing number of first-rate teachers. Things seemed to be charmed.

So it was not surprising that when Joan asked me to talk to her after lunch, I followed her into a bathroom with no apprehension. Playing with makeup at the mirror, we waited patiently for the room to clear. Finally we were alone.

"Carol, I have some bad news. I need you to forgive me," Joan began.

I searched her face, wondering what secret she may have let slip, still blissfully unconcerned.

"Scott and I are getting married," she said, voice faltering. Not catching the undertones, I smiled, thinking this to be a natural progression—good news to be fulfilled somewhere off in the distant future. Poor Joan. She must have wished for a smarter, more discerning friend. She was trying to break devastating news, and I was grinning like an idiot.

Giving up, she said, "I'm pregnant."

Words deserted me. Finally, looking past her to the row of stalls, I murmured, "For real?"

Today, in a different world, it is hard to explain my emotional state in November 1975. In those years, girls at our school did not get pregnant. It simply did not happen.

I stared at the floor, following the pattern of the gray and peach tiles. Stunned, unable to respond.

"Can you forgive me?" she asked, tears welling up.

"Of course," I replied, thinking that forgiveness was an odd thing to ask me for. "What can I do? How can I help?"

"You can pray for—"

I interrupted: "Do your parents know?" Joan nodded.

Finally, overwhelmed by the enormity of the situation, we hugged and cried together. "Mom and Dad are being great," she whispered.

"You are so lucky. My dad would kill him," I sighed.

"I thought my dad would too, but he's being pretty good so far."

Eventually Joan got to the details. There would be a wedding in ten days, a baby in late May. That night they would be going before their church and confessing their sin, begging forgiveness. That concept stopped me dead in my tracks. Confessing their sin? To the whole church? This sin? Sex outside marriage? My insides turned to Jell-O. Joan looked quite calm, giving me a peek into a spirit with more courage than most I would meet on earth.

"Uhhhh . . . at Hinson, right?" I asked.

Joan nodded. "It will be hard. Will you pray?"

"Absolutely." My mind worked at a super speed. Hinson Memorial Baptist Church. Not a member, I considered it one of the most imposing structures in the city. Hinson was a church with a prestigious history, a church that valued appearances. This was what I thought of Joan's church, but I had not met the true church at Hinson.

I walked home, skipping my afternoon classes. Sobbing, I opened the door and quickly fell into Mom's waiting arms. When she finally understood the source of my tears, she added her own.

Mom and I prayed for Joan and Scott, for their two families and for the church. Joan's family was generations deep at Hinson, her father a deacon. Scott, shy and gentle Scott, how would he survive the church confession, I wondered. Twenty-four hours later, the church had forgiven Joan and Scott and the process of redemption had begun.

Here's what happened: that Wednesday evening the family of God at Hinson entered the church building to be told that all meetings were canceled. There was trouble in the family, so all three or four hundred members would meet in the fellowship hall.

Pastor Baker solemnly opened the service. He reviewed principles of repentance and forgiveness, preparing a family to forgive. Finally he brought Scott and Joan, ages seventeen and eighteen, forward. They stood together, and Scott began to speak. Quietly and firmly he told the congregation that he and Joan had been dating for a year. They had become too involved and they had sinned. A baby was coming in the spring. Joan wept silently at his side.

Scott finished by telling the church that they had repented. They had received God's forgiveness and now they were asking the church to forgive them also—to support them in this difficult transition.

Pastor Baker moved between them, embracing both with an arm. "The leadership and I have forgiven them and stand with them," he said. "If you also forgive them I want you to stand up. Remember, as a Christian there can be no other response but forgiveness."

Telling me the story, Joan said it was as if everyone's seat had an electric shock attached to it. The congregation stood up immediately, loving completely, forgiving totally and being the pure and blameless bride of Christ. This was the true church, in all her glory.

In the ten days that followed, Joan was given two bridal showers. Four hundred people, none of whom had received the customary engraved invitation, attended her wedding. The crowd was so large they ran out of cake at the reception. A quick-thinking wedding coordinator ran to Albertsons and bought every sheet cake in sight. Joan and Scott are the only people I know who had a wedding cake decorated with a clown, balloons and "Happy Birthday, Billy!"

And God himself gave Joan a sweet remembrance of the day. She awoke on her wedding day to a light blanket of snow. It was not our usual weather in Portland, and it was absolutely beautiful. Lines from the old hymn, "Whiter than snow, yes whiter than snow—now wash me and I will be whiter than snow," ran through Joan's mind. God himself had come to visibly remind her that he had washed her. She was whiter than snow.

THE BENEFITS OF CONFESSION

Today Joan and I are sitting in a McDonald's sharing a midmorning Coke. She looks just like she did in 1976, but she is not the same person. She is twenty-some years wiser and richer, twenty-some years removed from the young woman who followed God with such determination and courage. And her spirit has only grown stronger.

"How's Karen?" I ask. Joan and Scott have four children, but Karen is the one I keep closest track of, the one whose birth feels like part of my own spiritual history.

Joan grins. "She's doing great at school. Broke all the time and thinks the guys are all dorks." I take exception. After all, my handsome and utterly charming nephew is at that college.

"Do you still get calls to talk to unwed mothers?" I ask. Joan and I have not talked about this in years.

Joan shakes her auburn head slowly. "Not often," she replies. "Usually, in today's world, people just expect us to accept a pregnancy or quietly abort the child."

"We grew up in a different world," I muse, amazed that the moral climate of the midseventies is so removed from that of the midnineties. I am amazed that we have traveled this far.

"Yes we did, and we are doing our daughters a disservice," Joan replies. "Today we all pretend that sin is no big deal—but the emotions, the penalty and the consequences have never changed. If we pretend they have, we are lying to our children. Confession brings a healing that the world cannot understand." Joan's voice is passionate, her body leaning decisively over the Formica tabletop.

"Once we confessed our sin, God was able to do amazing things. You know, after our public confession, I never felt guilt about it again. Guilt is just not allowed in forgiven sin. I was always proud of our baby."

"We all are proud of your baby," I add.

Joan continues. "Confession brought real peace. The kind of peace you need to live with—peace that affects your heart and your head."

"When did the healing process begin for you?" I ask.

"With acceptance by my parents," Joan answers quietly. Today, twenty years wiser, we are grateful for our parents.

"How did you tell them?" I wonder aloud, reliving the raw emotions of adolescence.

"Well, Scott and I had planned to tell them together, but the night before, I couldn't stand it. I thought I would burst. I went downstairs and crawled into bed with them and told them."

"What did they do?" I ask, wondering how Mark and I would respond.

"Mom wrapped me in her arms and my dad breathed heavy—very heavy for a long time," Joan says with a laugh. And together we giggle, twenty years removed from the pain. Twenty years of watching God form a family. But at the outset, her dad breathed heavy. Not a bad response, Mr. Milliken. Not bad at all!

"Really, the acceptance of God began for me with the acceptance of my parents. Then it trickled through the church. The response of the church became the physical manifestation of God for me. Their arms that hugged and held me became his arms."

"Isn't it glorious when the church is all she should be?" I ask.

"It is glorious. But don't glamorize my story, Carol. Scott and I both paid heavy prices. It's just that guilt wasn't one of them."

"Ummm. Wasn't Karen born during our Senior Breakfast?"

"Yes. May 21, 1976. I missed all of the activities I had so looked forward to. Not being part of the graduation ceremonies still hurts me," she admits. I look up quickly, surprised to find her eyes filling. I had no idea that the missed activities had hurt her so, which was foolish on my part. Joan had been slated for major roles in all of those activities.

"You know, Scott and I both had solid career plans that we never fulfilled. I was going to teach history and PE," she says.

"But you did teach, Joan!" I admonish. And over the next several moments she recalls how she was blessed to be a teacher for Bible Study Fellowship—teaching for three years and substituting for five. She taught 250 women each week, lecturing from the Scriptures. Having taught in high schools, I envy her because of her subject matter. "God does give back what the locusts have eaten," she admits, "but still the price of sin is unbelievably high."

Anxious to make us both feel better, I say, "And the treasure of confession is that all of us adore your child, knowing that she has the spiritual and moral courage of her mother and father!" I want badly for Joan to know how much I admire her and Scott. After all, God has used their lives to teach us about family, about the healing arms of God present in the local body, about the magic of turning dishonor into deep honor.

"You know," Joan says, "Karen Elizabeth means 'pure and consecrated to God.'"

We smile. We have twenty-some years of friendship to smile over.

So the toughest subpoint under confession was the first one I learned: some sins need to be confessed and forgiven by the church at large. Not all sins, but some. Joan and Scott were in a safe place to make such a confession. Their church had the maturity to act in accordance with the Scriptures.

Confession is an important part of working out one's salvation. I also feel we are called to be accountable to other human beings and to confess in repentance to them and whomever we harm by our sin. James instructs us to "confess your sins to each other and pray for each other so that you may be healed" (5:16). This practice certainly seems to have fallen out of vogue. Today I teach regularly on confession. There is power in finding a safe, older woman who loves God to confess my sin to. I find it makes me accountable and committed to repentance. It also frees me when I recognize that my older sister still loves me and so does God.

At least once each semester, I teach on the importance of finding a trustworthy spiritual mentor to confess your sins to. I recommend finding older, wiser Christians who can be trusted with a confidence. When a student asks me to hear a confession of sin, we always do so in prayer. Following the student's acknowledgment of sin, I have learned to say, "And Lord, you know that I am also guilty."

This may seem a strange habit. It certainly was for me. Confessing is strange, because it is strange for a person to openly admit wrongdoing. It is equally strange for hearers to admit that they also are guilty—when they may not have committed the identical sin. It is important that those who hear another's confession recognize that they too stand knee-deep in the grungy stuff called sin. We have a common fallen nature, we have a common struggle, and we are all guilty of sin. It does not need to be identical sin. My conscience may be clear of your sin, but that does not make me innocent.

CORPORATE CONFESSION

Over the years, I have come to love the *Book of Common Prayer.* The first time I attended a liturgical church, I was driven to tears by the words and events surrounding the confession of sin. The congregation, from the least to the priest, kneels together and says these words,

> Most merciful God,
> We confess that we have sinned against you
> In thought, word, and deed,
> By what we have done,
> And by what we have left undone.
> We have not loved you with our whole heart;
> We have not loved our neighbors as ourselves.
> We are truly sorry and we humbly repent.
> For the sake of your Son Jesus Christ,
> Have mercy on us and forgive us;
> That we may delight in your will,
> And walk in your ways,
> To the glory of Your Name. Amen.

And doesn't that prayer cover it all, as the church confesses individually and corporately? What we have done and what we have left undone. Those times when we have not loved God or humanity with our whole heart.

This is the prayer I use daily, quieting myself prior to the words, searching for the individual events that have grieved the heart of God. The prayer is a constant. Each evening when I approach it, I find areas to clean up. I have never had a sin-free day. I assume that this prayer, this confession, will always be part of my days on earth. If it fails to be so, it will not be because I am perfect, but because I have fallen away.

I have a set of questions I use to jolt my heart and make way for confession. If your spirit needs a jumpstart in this discipline, try these questions. Most of us cannot get past number one without falling to our knees. And our knees are a wonderful place to fall to. May yours also bend before him.

QUESTIONS FOR EXAMINING YOUR CONSCIENCE

- Have I doubted God? Have I despaired of his goodness? Have I failed to recognize his loving work in my life?

- Have I been truthful? Have my words hurt the reputations of others? Have I been honest with God?

- Have I treated others with respect? Have I been careful to consider others more highly than myself?

- Have I acted in anger in ways that hurt others or damaged the reputation of Christ and his church? Have I held onto anger? Have I refused to forgive others?

- Have I taken care of my body? Am I a faithful steward of the temple of the Holy Spirit?

- Have I kept the Lord's Day?

- Have I kept myself sexually pure in thought, word and deed?

- Have I failed to act in loving ways with my family? My friends? My coworkers?

- Have I failed to promote unity in the body of Christ?

- Have I been faithful to my conscience?

I seldom get past point one. But it is a useful tool, one I use regularly and am honored to pass on. May you join my sisters and me as we kneel and come clean.

FOR REFLECTION AND DISCUSSION

1. How has confession been used in your life? In the lives of women you admire?

2. What does Scripture teach about confession? Use these references as a jumping-off spot:
   - 1 John 1:8-9
   - James 5:16

3. Quietly review questions for the examination of conscience found on the final pages of this chapter. Allow the Holy Spirit to prompt you in your silent confession to God.

Teach Me to Forgive

. . . .

The teachers of the law and the Pharisees brought in a woman caught in adultery. They made her stand before the group and said to Jesus, "Teacher, this woman was caught in the act of adultery. In the Law Moses commanded us to stone such women. Now what do you say?" They were using this question as a trap, in order to have a basis for accusing him.

But Jesus bent down and started to write on the ground with his finger. When they kept on questioning him, he straightened up and said to them, "If any one of you is without sin, let him be the first to throw a stone at her." Again he stooped down and wrote on the ground.

JOHN 8:3-8

THE ADULTERESS'S STORY

It has been four years and still the nightmares wake him. My little boy is growing now into the body of a man and he continues to wake, screaming for his mother, terrified of the stones that never flew. My poor child, haunted by a mother's guilt and the angry righteousness of guilty men.

My sin is a nightmare we continue to live with daily. Everyone knows. Everyone. It is easy to see which young girl has just been told my story. She blushes when her eyes meet mine. Imagine, an adulteress, right here in the village. Caught in the act . . . that is the piece that sends their imagination winging and their blush deepening.

It is not as if we planned adultery. My husband was dead. A drunkard—it was hard to grieve him. I wore the clothes of a widow, kept the religious customs of widowhood, but my heart did not conform. I was grateful that he was gone. Grateful that my children and I would never again work to hide bruises that were the results of his love affair with drink. Grateful that he could no longer hurt us.

So, when Thomas returned to town, returned with an invalid wife, it is small wonder that my heart began to pound. He had been my playmate as a child, my eight-year-old defender. He had begged Father to allow him to marry me, but Father saw only the money my husband had to offer as a bride price. Thomas could not match the cash. But fifteen years after my marriage, Thomas returned.

Thomas.

Handsome to my eyes. Smiling a smile that was as familiar to me as my mother's. Laughing, cajoling, understanding. Thomas, twin to my soul.

We did not set out to commit adultery. We were circumspect at first. If he had not known me so well, known my expressions. If we had not moved close enough to touch. . . . Well, it is finished. We did know each other well; we did touch.

They dragged me before another religious teacher. My four children looked on, sobbing in fear. I longed to comfort them. What kind of mother risks her children's future for the love of an old friend? What kind of mother was I? What kind of mother am I?

The teacher seemed uninterested. I was just another sinner. One more caught in the net. One more destined for the pit outside town. And all the while I begged God to send someone to take my children. Someone to shield their eyes.

The teacher bent down and began to write in the dirt. I cannot read. I did not know what he was writing. Glancing around, I realized that the teachers of the law had fallen silent. Many of the older ones were flushed. A red stain crept up their faces. And still the teacher wrote.

Then the younger men were looking away. I searched the horizon, wondering what they were looking at—or for. What had the teacher written?

"If any one of you is without sin, let him be the first to throw a stone at her," Jesus said.

One by one the rocks dropped to the ground. But this one, this Jesus—even if all the others turned away, surely this man could throw a rock. Surely he was without sin.

Standing, Jesus addressed me. "Woman, where are they? Has no one condemned you?"

"No one, sir," I answered. The children drew close. Our tears streamed as one. My littlest, Jonah, seven years old, sobbed and hiccupped behind me.

"Then neither do I condemn you," Jesus said. "Go now, and leave your life of sin."

I could not believe my ears. How could this man forgive me? How could he allow me to go? I wiped my cheeks with the heels of my hands. "I can go? You forgive me?" I asked.

The teacher smiled. It was a kind smile. I began to wonder: Did he somehow know it all—Thomas, the bride price? Did he know the whole, complicated mess? He nodded toward my children, his voice kind. "Go, woman. Sin no more."

So my life was spared, but my children, especially poor little Jonah, will never be the same. He is haunted by my sin and the leaders holding stones in their hands. He is terrified and I cannot soothe him.

I feel bitter about those old men in their religious robes. They were not without sin. They only stopped because Jesus wrote in the dirt.

Whatever he wrote, he reminded them of their own sin. Those old men mock me; they sneer in disgust. They sigh and pick up their robes lest our common dirt contaminate them.

And still the voice of Jesus lingers in my ears: "If anyone is without sin . . ." "Forgive, and you will be forgiven." His teaching can be so hard. I must forgive my prosecutors? I must forgive those men who shielded Thomas yet pushed my children to the front to observe their mother's shame? How can I forgive someone who has not asked for forgiveness? People whose very presence terrifies my child?

And yet, Jesus forgave me. He spared my life. No, those old men in their religious robes hold no fear for me. It is Jesus who haunts my dreams, begging me to forgive.

· · · · · · ·

LEARNING TO FORGIVE

Forgiveness is the lesson that separates the serious followers of Jesus from the wannabees. It is the most difficult lesson of all, one we are taught from the cross of Christ. In my own journey, the Lord had me work on confession for two solid years before he began the truly difficult work of teaching me the deep lessons of forgiveness. When it was time to learn, he again enlisted the help of that circle of women who had mentored and nurtured me throughout my young adulthood.

As a child I had learned how to mouth the words of forgiveness. I had learned how to forgive my sister for playing with my dolls. I had learned how to put on a pious face to fool my mother. I had not learned how to truly forgive.

As a young adult, I had layers of hurts and resentments in my life. I was bitterly angry over some of those hurts, and forgiveness was the furthest thing from my mind and my heart. For me, forgiveness sounded horribly vulnerable. I was interested in self-preservation, not forgiving.

Enter the sisterhood of believers—kind, compassionate women who saw a caged animal and determined to set it free. These women knew and understood that I preferred the cage of resentment and hurt to freedom. They had lived in cages themselves and knew that the freedom of forgiveness, the freedom of a self held captive by the gospel, is always preferable to the cage of self-preservation.

My sisters had a lesson for me, a lesson I was not terribly interested in learning. At this point in my life, I had just spent two years learning to live in a state of daily confession. If I had put all of that enormous spiritual and psychological effort into learning confession, it was high time the rest of the church caught up. I wasn't about to learn forgiveness until they learned confession. Self-preservation sounded essential to me. Forgiveness sounded terrifying.

I had been in an intense study of the Word for almost a year when my mentors recommended that I pray and fast, asking the Lord for a list of the people whom I needed to forgive. I did not think much of their assignment. I avoided it. I learned to respond with carefully chosen words that sounded like I was moving right along when I was actually at a dead, full stop. In other words, I lied. I avoided them and I avoided Jesus. Like the woman caught in adultery, I was haunted by Jesus' command to forgive. I tried desperately to forget that command.

THE CHURCH

At this point, Mark and I had spent four long years in a church that viewed women as nursery workers and kitchen attendants. These restrictive roles for women had been formed by centuries of believers who took literally Paul's command for women to learn in silence. I was allowed to partner with my husband in running children's ministries, but it was Mark they would listen to.

I had groaned often under the weight of these restrictions. This church did not know what to make of Genesis 1—"in the image of God . . . male and female he created them." Yet God had called us there.

It was an ongoing private pain for me and occasionally a public pain for both Mark and me. In our position as head of children's ministries, Mark and I were given full access to the elder board. We found that my ideas, my visions, were best expressed through Mark. If he articulated my ideas, the men on the board found them easier to assimilate. They paid closer attention when Mark spoke. This wounded me deeply. I often awoke with tears on my cheeks, my spirit torn.

For years our elder board had stated publicly that they wanted to see women use the gifts God had given them, and they were disappointed to see a lack of response. They wanted women to be active in the life of the church, but found women less and less willing to participate in those silent roles assigned to them by custom. They did not understand that their own view of women kept many from participating.

Those men loved the women of our church—not perfectly, but sincerely and faithfully. They wished I was not hurting, that none of us were hurting. They too wanted healing for the body of Christ. That January, our elder board took action. They called on an elder from a church back east, a close friend of our pastor, and invited him to come in late January and teach for three days on the role of women in the church.

Hearing that a man was being summoned to teach women their place, I struggled with a choice: rebellion or reform? Is my anger righteous indignation that will lead to reform, or is it rebellion? Like most powerful moves of God, reform has a counterfeit. It can be hard to tell which is which. At some point in the struggle it occurred to me: *What if this man, this male, is sent from God?* With that thought, I moved as quickly as I could from frustration to prayer: "Lord, what is your will in all of this?"

THE SISTERS

The next night I returned to my Bible study group. There my kind, wonderful sisters were eager to talk it out. They were willing to listen to all of me—the anger and frustration, the prayers, the questions about my own heart.

In this small group, not everyone shared my convictions about women. Two were content with the way things were and wondered what the fuss was all about. One was as immersed in the fuss as I was. But the issue did not separate us. They loved me, right or wrong, pure or fallen, rebelling or reforming. And in that atmosphere of love I was free to grow, free to work through this deepest hurt.

We agreed that I would spend the next week chronicling my hurts. We had learned the importance of looking honestly at hurts—looking, analyzing, confessing, repenting and forgiving on a daily basis. I was able to forgive small hurts, but these were deep aches I was nursing.

These sisters of mine were determined. Regardless of the pain involved, I was to look at this carefully guarded area of my life involving women in the church. I would look, analyze, confess my own sin, repent of my sin and forgive those others at fault. Surrounded by a trinity of strong, loving women, I had no out. I had to do my work. Like the woman taken in adultery, I would need to forgive just as I had been forgiven.

The week zoomed by. I wrote and wrote and wrote. The morning of the seminar, I finished my homework: twenty-plus pages of pain. Only then did the Spirit of God come and make himself known, whispering to me, "Now we will begin the process of restoration." Wonderful words of life! Restoration! Restore me! My spirit sang out the words in trusting abandon.

RESTORATION BEGINS WITH FORGIVENESS

The three-day seminar was filled with joy. The teacher affirmed both males and females. He saw both as having God-given attributes that are needed in the body of Christ. He honored all. I do not know if our elders were surprised by his teaching. They exchanged smiles occasionally but made no public comment. Nor did the basic structure of the church change. It was only the beginning, the spark that could be seen in many individual faces.

Mark and I were instructed, affirmed and encouraged by his teaching, and by Sunday morning we were beaming. But for me the smile had a strange counterpart. Somewhere deep inside me, I was angry. Why? Why, when a wonderful teacher had affirmed the dignity of women and honored women for three straight days?

As the service ended, the teacher was praying over individuals. My sisters came and found me unsettled. They empathized, putting loving arms around me. No one had an answer for my bewildering emotions. Finally I joined the line of those needing prayer. When the teacher reached me, I explained that I was angry. His answer was immediate and painfully clear: "You need to forgive."

I was aghast. *Forgive? Twenty-plus pages of grief and I need to forgive? No, dear brother! They need to repent.*

Silently we viewed each other. He was well aware of my hesitation. "Let's do it now. Put an end to it today," he said, smiling encouragement. I liked this man. I liked him a lot. He was cut from the same fine cloth as my husband and my father. I didn't want to disappoint him. And unlike my circle of sisters—sympathetic to the end—this man was demanding that we conquer the problem.

"Okay," I said, hardly aware of the decision being made. "Lord, help me to forgive—"

He interrupted. "Nope." I had never been interrupted in prayer. My eyes asked the question. "You don't need help," he explained. "You need to forgive. Take another stab at it." His hand rested on my shoulder. I felt like a high jumper getting instructions from the coach.

Nodding, I returned to the work. "Lord, I need to forgive—"

"Nope."

The interruptions were beginning to unnerve me. *Who is this man and what does he want from me?* I glanced up to find tender eyes watching me. His person was reflecting clearly the Lord I love so much. "Okay. I'm not getting it," I admitted. "What am I doing wrong?"

He smiled. "You don't want to, need to or require help to forgive. You need to state, simply, that you *do* forgive."

"Umm . . ." This man, directed by my Lord, meant business. There would be no nice escape. The poison of anger, bitterness and resentment was going to be removed or I would have to admit that I wanted to keep them as companions—and hang forgiveness. The choice was mine.

"Right," I stammered, feeling the emotions tighten my throat and blur my vision.

"Let's nail it," he said, ever the coach, determined to get the athlete over the high bar.

I braced myself and finally began my trek down the track. "Lord, I have not forgiven as you forgave." The pat on my shoulder assured me that I was on my way. No interruptions this round. "Lord, I forgive . . ." The names rolled off my tongue and released me from my tomb. Stones of unforgiveness, blocking the light, were removed. The clear bright light of resurrection grew visible at a distance.

As I finished, the teacher/coach took over. "Lord, I stand as her witness, that on this day, she did indeed forgive these sins committed against her. Whenever the enemy would try to get her to recall them, to embrace them, to make them residents in her life, remind her of this day. You and I are witnesses to her work."

The work of forgiveness was complete. His words removed the temptation to disavow the work of God in my life. From that day forward, I had a witness who would stand with me, or testify against me should I deny the work of God in my life, should I try to reclaim the anger and the bitterness. What a mentor! What a lesson!

THE LESSON

I had no idea that forgiveness would be part of the restoring of my soul. Yet forgiveness brought me back to a place of purity. I felt clean inside. I had never before understood the entrapping power of failing to forgive or the profound peace that comes with forgiving.

The placement of this lesson in my adult life was no mistake. It followed two years of being asked by God to learn to live in a daily state of confession. Finally confession had more or less become a habit. Now I needed to study forgiveness.

Why had God asked me to focus on confession first? A powerful statement from A. Boyce Gibson helped me understand: "The only people who can be trusted with forgiveness are those who at the same time acknowledge their solidarity in sin with the forgiven. Otherwise, forgiveness, like justice, is an instrument of oppression."

First I needed to know, deep in my bones, that I am a sinner. I am firmly entrenched in a fallen world as a fallen individual in need of the daily saving power of Jesus Christ. Then the logical step was learning to forgive. Once I was convinced of my own sin, forgiveness withheld would have been blasphemy.

My head understood the logic. My heart cried out for easier lessons.

FORGIVE US AS WE FORGIVE

It was just weeks later that I heard Father Richard Treadwell speak on Matthew 6:12: "Forgive us our debts, as we also have forgiven our debtors." He talked about his own problems with that verse—how his flesh wants to see the bad guys get what's coming to them, how he never wishes the same punishment on himself. Then he went on to say, "Our sins are forgiven with the same energy and thoroughness that we forgive others."

Stop the sermon. Obviously Treadwell's seminary wasn't kosher. Someone had taught him wrong. I am forgiven. What is this nonsense about only being forgiven with the same energy and thoroughness that I forgive others? That's not in the Bible. Not in my version.

I went home disgruntled. Then the quiet voice of a sister came. Having been raised Catholic, Wendy said, "Why don't you let the whole thing rest for a few days. Just say the Lord's Prayer over and over. Pretend you are a good Catholic." I could hear the amusement in her voice.

"Just the Lord's Prayer?" I asked.

"Yeah," she said. "Give yourself a rest. Bathe yourself in prayer, the prayer Jesus used to teach us to pray."

It sounded good to me. And so I began, day after day, over and over. "Forgive us our trespasses as we forgive those who trespass against us." The line stood out in stark relief. Just what had Jesus meant? Wasn't it just that I was to put forth a good effort every so often? I returned to my Bible to find out. Matthew wrote, "For if you forgive men when they sin against you, your heavenly Father will also forgive you. But if you do not forgive men their sins, your Father will not forgive your sins" (6:14-15). Ouch.

My forgiveness is conditional on my willingness to forgive others. Not just willingness—active forgiveness. These verses made me most uncomfortable. They erased my picture of a "say these words and everything is cool" type of God. My God, Jesus his Son, was commanding forgiveness.

I looked further into Scripture. Mark 11:25 was crystal clear: "And when you stand praying, if you hold anything against anyone, forgive him, so that your Father in heaven may forgive you your sins." Luke 6:37 reads, "Do not judge, and you will not be judged. Do not condemn, and you will not be condemned. Forgive, and you will be forgiven." If anything, the teachings of Jesus were becoming progressively harder.

I began to wonder if he had read the headlines of the *Oregonian* lately. Did he understand the sins of the twenty-first century: sexual abuse, date rape, insider trading, serial killing? Did he understand what it was like to be a mother in this crazy society? Did he know the fear?

I went on to the next reference in my concordance, Luke 23:33-34: "When they came to the place called the Skull, there they crucified him, along with the criminals—one on his right, the other on his left. Jesus said, 'Father, forgive them, for they do not know what they are doing.' And they divided up his clothes by casting lots."

Suffering an unbelievably cruel death, Jesus who knew no sin forgave his murderers as they gambled for his clothes. His mother was there. He knew her pain. It added untold weight to his own.

This picture forever destroyed my comfortable picture of Christianity. It also destroyed my newfound reason to forgive: forgive to be forgiven. It had seemed logical. It had begun to make sense—until I came to the place of the Skull, until I viewed my Lord hanging on raw lumber, gasping for breath yet pushing out words of forgiveness. He knew no sin. He had no real reason to forgive, no quid pro quo to satisfy.

New to the paths of forgiveness, my spirit rebelled. I did not like the Christ-established model. I wanted better bookkeeping. Can you understand the careful bookkeeping I was looking for? It is a matter of other people acknowledging the devastation that their sin has caused while I call mine a "white lie." It means that there were valid reasons for my misconduct, while others were guilty of malicious sin. It means that my sin was minor and another's sin was the nail that pierced my Savior's hand.

Jesus has ways of dealing with bookkeepers. He let me run through all my mazes, play intellectual games, justify, rationalize, downplay my own involvement. Then, when my spirit was finally quiet, he gave me a mental picture. It was a picture of him. Jesus came into my room, sat down on a kitchen stool and turned his back to me. Slowly, seriously, he removed the white shirt he wore. There, before my unhappy eyes, was his battered back, crisscrossed with the lashings of a Roman military unit. Puffy, red scar tissue. The lashings meshed together, one large disfiguring mass.

He beckoned me to touch it. Hesitantly, gently, my fingers traced the scars. My hands trembled and the teeth that clenched my lower lip would not relax.

"Now," he said, his eyes serious and kind, "show me which ones are yours."

As long as I live, I will not forget the day or the picture. My sins. Meshed with all of humanity's. Impossible to separate. Impossible to ignore. Now that battered back stands as a bond between me and my brothers and sisters. No individual sin is discernible. All are guilty.

And the tenderness of Jesus' eyes remains with me also. Forgiveness is forever etched on his back. Love continually shines forth from his eyes. Who am I to deny either?

THE HARSH AND HEALING REALITY

I learned the harsh and healing reality of forgiveness when I was teaching a Bible study. It was a warm August evening and I had taught the group my own lesson of forgiveness. It was a good lesson; the women were moved and the presence of the Lord graced our living room. I finished with my best illustration, paused and closed my Bible, intending to pray.

"Carol?" a small voice asked. I looked up to see Grace. She is not quite five feet tall, entering her fifties, struggling with weight problems. Grace seldom spoke in our class. If she had a question, I was more than happy to hear it.

"Yes?"

"Well, Carol, I like what you have to say and all, but sometimes you can't always forgive people when they are alive."

I watched Grace carefully. She sat very still, head bowed, hands clenched. Her feet barely reached the floor. Her statement left me in a quandary. When you are the youngest woman in the room and also the teacher, you learn quickly to embrace silence and listen to experience. I did not want my lesson watered down, but I did want Grace to have a safe place to speak, to share her own stories, something she had not yet done.

"Can you explain for us?" I asked. Grace's head slowly rose. Her eyes met mine. "Yes, I can explain," she said. The room was silent. Each one wanted to hear her story, and each one was forever changed by the story we heard.

"I was the youngest of ten children," she began. "My oldest sister was twenty-three when I was born. I had nephews and nieces older than me.

"My father hated women. He used to say, 'All women are whores, boys; that's what they're made for.' This is how he instructed my brothers. From the time I was five until my menstrual cycle started at ten, my brothers sexually abused me." The living room was deathly still. The Kleenex box began its trek around the silent circle.

"When I was little, I used to hide under the dining room table. It had a long tablecloth on it and I felt safe there. I learned to count the big feet as they went by so I would know when it was safe to come out. My parents did nothing to protect us. My sister and I told my mother. She did nothing. We had no door on our bedroom. Even a door would have helped us. But they did nothing.

"My father died when I was seventeen. I did not grieve.

"As an adult, I finally found Jesus. He began to heal me," her voice wavered for the first time. Several pairs of hands reached out to squeeze hers. Struggling, she went on. "I felt like a tramp. You see, I too had learned my father's lesson well.

"My coming to Jesus had all kinds of miracles attached to it. At every step, he assured me that I was clean. Not a tramp, but a daughter. Not a whore, but a bride.

"Eventually, as I neared forty, I knew I had to do something about my anger. Jesus had answered my prayer. He had allowed me to see myself in the mirror of another person. A person filled with anger. I did not like what I saw. I would have to allow him to be Lord in this area too.

"So I decided to forgive my father and brothers. I had moved two thousand miles from home. It was time to go back. My sister and I visited home for a relative's wedding. I made a list of all Dad's wrongs. Then I borrowed a car and drove to the cemetery where Dad was buried. Kneeling by the grave, I used my fingers to dig up a small patch of ground. I buried my father's sins with him and left them there.

"I had been so angry. Now the anger was gone. It didn't own me. Kneeling by the grave, I said, 'There, Dad. It's done.' Two strong hands gripped my shoulders and pulled me up. Amazingly, a priest had come. He was not someone I knew and no one knew where I was. Only God could have sent him.

"This kind priest put his arms around me and said, 'You're right. It is done. It's over. Leave it there.' I turned back to the grave, encouraged by this kind man of God. 'It's over, Daddy. It's all done. I forgive you.'

"I turned around to thank the priest, but he was gone. I stood up and looked around, but I could not see him anywhere."

"What do you mean?" one woman asked.

"I mean, the priest had disappeared. Into thin air. Gone," Grace said with a smile. "But not before his work was done. You see, I couldn't forgive my father when he was alive because he did not want to be forgiven and I did not want to forgive. Once I met Jesus, and Jesus was so good, I had to forgive."

Shaky smiles filled my living room. Yes, once you meet Jesus, and Jesus is so good, you have to forgive. You have to do anything your Lord commands. Meeting Jesus. Seeing the goodness. Forgiveness made easier. Forgiveness made real. Forgiveness brought by the true High Priest.

FOR REFLECTION AND DISCUSSION

1. Who has taught you lessons of forgiveness? What lessons in forgiving have you learned that you could pass on?

2. Receiving forgiveness from God for our own sins comes with a responsibility. Read the following verses and explain the believer's responsibility to forgive.

   • Matthew 6:12, 14
   • Mark 11:25
   • Luke 6:37

3. Spend some moments in prayerful meditation. Who are the people you have refused to forgive? Are there areas of your own life that feel unforgiven? Take a few moments, and in prayer, forgive.

Support in Seasons
of Grief and Hope

. . . .

Mary Magdalene went to the disciples with the news:
"I have seen the Lord!"

JOHN 20:18

MARY MAGDALENE'S STORY

We stood together as a group that Friday afternoon. Women are not common spectators at crucifixions. We stood silent, unable to take into our beings the picture before our eyes.

He hung in great pain, no different from any man or woman who had undergone the torment of the Romans. They had stripped him, thinking to humiliate the prophet, not realizing that the Creator is never embarrassed by the creature he has created.

Sometime after three, he cried out in a loud voice. A shudder ran through our small congregation. Now the tears that shock had shielded ran like streams down our faces. Now the convulsions of grief shook our bodies.

It was finished. He who had healed me could not, or would not, save himself.

I wanted to stride over the hills with my fists shaking at God. I wanted to yell and scream away the injustice. I wanted to rend heaven with my rage. But my body would not obey. Instead I held the slumping body of his mother, and I mothered her. I whispered comfort, feeling none. I rocked her and keened with her. Finally I lifted her to her feet and took her to his body.

Joseph, an honorable religious man, came to offer help. He had a new grave. He would take the body there. Mary cradled her son in her arms. I nodded our acceptance.

Somehow I thought he was as much mine as hers. I had loved her son with an intensity few experience. Not sexually, as the gossip mongers would have you think . . . but purely, with a joy and innocence no one thought me capable of.

So Mary and I buried her son.

Mary's movements were mechanical and held no thought. Gone were the sparks in her eyes. I worried over her. It is not good for grief to go too silent. Yet there is a sweetness in the heart of God. It never ceases to amaze me, to comfort me, to sustain in the midst of our greatest pain.

The Sabbath prevented the burial from being completed. Unable to obtain the necessary spices and winding clothes so late on a Friday, Mary and I had simply lain the body, with a burial cloth on it, in the tomb. We would return with the proper ointments and perfumes on Sunday.

Pilate sealed the tomb, fearing the disciples. That one gave me cynical amusement. Eleven terrified men. Scattered to the corners of the city. Hiding out in basements and attics. And Pilate thought them capable of theft.

On Sunday, Mary could not face it. She had not spoken since the cross. She had not cried. She had not slept. She sat silent in the darkness, rocking back and forth, humming lullabies. Derangement was only footsteps away.

I gathered the items and went to the tomb.

All my life I had heard of God's displeasure. How God held all women responsible for the Eden fiasco. How men were the chosen ones. All my life I believed this.

But somewhere, in my heart of hearts, I held out hope. This same Jesus who had cared for me—this Son of God who had delivered me—caused me to wonder: might not God love women as fiercely as we love God? My answer came that morning.

An empty tomb. A woman, and yet I was the first to see an empty tomb.

Now, it is true, I did not understand it, but who would? I had carried and laid out a corpse. I knew he was dead. I had seen the changes a body endures when the spirit departs. His skin had yellowed like all dead things. His eyes had glazed. His face had ceased to be the Jesus we all knew.

So an empty tomb is not understandable.

But that loving heart of God . . . a voice, a question, and then a name. My name. Mary. He called out my name. The world would never be the same; grief would never hold the same pain. All because of an empty tomb and the calling of a woman's name.

· · · · · · ·

SEASONS OF GRIEF

Grief. Loss. Those moments change our worlds forever. C. S. Lewis once said, "Grief is like the sky; it covers everything." Yes, grief does cover everything. And each time we are bereaved, each time our world is devastated by loss, we feel the craziness of it all. We do not understand, we can't reason out the "why," but like the sky, the loss is everywhere. It is during these seasons that mentors are the difference between living again and quietly closing up shop.

Mary Magdalene knew that grief. She continues to mentor us through Scripture, changing our lives two thousand years after her own death. She had not only lost a friend; she had lost all hope. Isn't it wonderful to realize that God entrusted women with such amazing messages? One Mary was the first to know that he was coming to earth; another was the first to know that he had risen. They understood the wonderful hope our faith supplies. They also knew the seasons of grief.

In the spring of 1994, my fifty-seven-year-old mother was told she had a deadly form of cancer. Extremely rare, only one in ten people survive its first year.

My mother had always been my closest female friend. She had mothered me, mentored me and loved me. Her mother lived into her seventies and her aunts survived well into their eighties. I was unprepared to lose my mother in her fifties.

For two years, Mom did extremely well. Then in the summer of 1996, she went home where she met her Savior face to face. She finally put sight to the voice she'd embraced. It was a holy time, a birth more than a death, and we released her with both joy and sorrow.

It took me years to adjust to living without Mom, to celebrate the joys of this life with the shadow of the cross as a constant companion. My mother's passing is still a part of my daily thoughts. Each night I remind the Lord of the treasure he holds.

In that dark and shadowed valley of grief, my sisters again guided me, marking our paths with tears, sobs and gasps of unexpected joy and hope. I was the uninitiated, grateful recipient of their difficult spiritual work. My own story is only complete in the light of theirs.

Worship Heals

During my first year of teaching high school English, sorrow and loss seemed as distant as Neptune and Pluto. At twenty-three, the worst I could imagine was losing my dog. I had learned that boyfriends come and go, but a good lapdog is a comfort forever.

That year, a family in our church lost a sixteen-year-old daughter in a car accident. In the blink of an eye, a dearly loved girl left her father and mother and journeyed home to her Savior. I did not know the family well—only by sight—but they would teach me one of the most important lessons in how to survive grief and loss.

I did not spend hours contemplating their sorrow. Like most people, I found it easier to murmur platitudes, promise prayer and forget it all as quickly as possible. I was unaware that I too had a lesson to learn.

On the Sunday morning after Friday's tragedy, the mother and father were in church. Today I realize that there is great strength and comfort in the community of believers. Then I was simply stunned that anyone would go out in public so soon.

But there they were. Al is about five ten and stocky. He looks like a wrestling coach, all energy and power in the shape of a block. His red-brown hair caps off incredible energy. Next to him was his wife, Andy, almost as tall as her husband, slender, with shoulder-length blonde hair and large soulful eyes. While Al is the picture of strength, Andy is wraithlike. Her hands are delicate, her limbs slender, her eyes large and deep-set.

I should have known that a wraith married to a powerhouse would have unbelievable reserves of her own. I cannot recall the songs we sang that morning, but I'll never forget the picture of grace and faith that was given me that morning. There in the third row, two days after their child's death, Al and Andy praised God. His powerful arms and her slender, delicate ones were lifted heavenward. Empty arms expressing spirits full of trust and hope.

When Mother was dying, remembering those arms raised in tenacious, faith-filled worship gave me hope. Hope that arms and hands and entire beings can still be full of faith and gifted with grace.

THANKSGIVING HEALS

Sally comes to my Monday night class. She hungers after God.

Sally warned me early on that she might not wish to share much in class. Three years earlier, as she entered her forties, she had lost a son to bone cancer. She knew that public discussion of her own spiritual journey was likely to leave her in tears, and she had already cried enough.

There is something about the loss of a child that causes other mothers to pull back. It is not a conscious action but a shutting down of what is too painful to contemplate. Psychologists call it distancing. If we put space between ourselves and another's pain, it cannot happen to us. This is not logical, but it is a normal response, one that lightens our load and increases the pain and loneliness of the bereaved.

Two years into the Monday night class, I still knew very little about Sally's loss. Her tears were never far from the surface, so I knew the pain remained. Finally she and I were left alone one evening, and she graciously told me her story.

A year and a half before their son Vaughn's diagnosis, Lloyd and Sally lived in a lovely suburban home. Sally had designed it and loved every inch of it. Being a house-lover myself, I understand intimately the tie a person can have to a house. Sally and Lloyd had three thriving children, Vaughn, Shauna and Melissa.

But the family-owned business was in trouble. A business bankruptcy followed and Lloyd had to find a new job. Then suddenly he was transferred to another state. Much as it hurt them, they put the house on the market and prepared to move. The house sold the first day it was listed. But two weeks before the closing, Lloyd lost his job. Depressed, he began searching for work. Depression for individuals in sales is not a prescription for success. Struggling, Lloyd soon questioned his desire to be a husband. The responsibility was too great— the fear of failure too strong. At this point Sally thought she'd reached the bottom. Nothing else could go wrong.

In August the family moved into an apartment where the kids could continue in their previous schools. On September 13, Vaughn was diagnosed with bone cancer. He was thirteen and a half years old. True bone cancer is extremely rare. It affects the actual bone and most often afflicts boys during their main growth years.

They began the school year with Vaughn having a fifty-fifty chance. Vaughn had five sessions of chemotherapy that fall. The treatments involved hospital stays. In December, surgeons removed his thigh bone and knee joint in an eleven-hour surgery. As soon as he recovered from the surgery, the chemo began again. The family remained hopeful.

In May, cancer was found in Vaughn's shoulder and both lungs. The doctors told them it was hopeless. The only thing left to try was highly experimental. Vaughn wanted to fight, so they flew to the National Institutes of Health, where he underwent a new treatment. No luck. On August 15, 1991, just eleven months after diagnosis, Vaughn left this earth.

Sally is very composed as she tells me her story. We sit in the living room of her new home in the suburbs of Portland. It is a pretty room, neat and lovingly cared for. The walls have pictures of her three children and several other kids I do not recognize. Vaughn's brown eyes shine at us from a nearby frame. He is a handsome kid, tall, with the frame of an athlete who is just getting his growth. His smile is as clean and white and all-American as Brad Pitt's.

I look at the photo of this vibrantly alive young man and cannot see him as anything but living. It occurs to me that this is just fine, because Vaughn will live forever. Not in our memories, but in a realm we acknowledge but cannot touch. Vaughn has departed the shadowlands of this life for real life, for eternal life.

Sally watches me look at the picture of her son. Tears come and go.

"Sally, when you knew . . . I mean, when you really knew you were losing him, were you angry at God?" I ask, keenly aware that there is within me a deep anger about my mother's death that is still unresolved. After all, God is God. God can do anything. And Mom was a wonderful, godly woman who should still be delighting us at eighty. Vaughn was a super kid. His mom should be telling me about his latest mischief, not his funeral. I needed to pull her experience into my own pain so I could learn from her.

"Angry?" she muses. "At times." Her smile is sad. "I was angry at Vaughn that he couldn't fight harder, that he wasn't winning. I was angry at myself, because I felt I should have been able to pray harder. We teach that God answers prayer, but we often forget that God does not always say yes. I was angry at Lloyd for the insecurities we had lived through and were still living through. I wondered if the stress had caused the cancer. But mostly I was just disappointed. Disappointed with God and lonely. Terribly lonely."

I wonder how many of my questions are cruel. She has offered me her story, offered to teach me the lessons she has clawed out of the granite of grief. All the same, I wonder what is fair. My silence encourages her.

"You know," she goes on, "right up to the last few days, I never thought Vaughn would die. I always thought God would perform a miracle. But looking back, I think Vaughn knew. I think he had begun to distance himself."

"How did Vaughn handle all of this?" I wonder aloud.

"He was amazing." The pride in her voice is bittersweet for me. I can tell that she adored this young man. "He hated the hospital. So on the way there for a treatment, I asked him if he was angry at God. He never hesitated. Just said no. He used to reassure both Lloyd and me. Used to tell us that 'God will take care of it.'"

I sit quietly, amazed and humbled at the strength of a thirteen-year-old. "How did you and Lloyd stay together?" I ask, fearing more pain.

"We knew the statistics for divorce after losing a child were incredibly high. The kids had been through so much already, so we recommitted our marriage to God. But it has been lonely. We still can't help each other much. The mother-son relationship is so different from the father-son relationship; it was like we lost different people, both named Vaughn.

"I miss my son. No one talks about the sweetness of the mother-son relationship."

Sally's eyes brim over. While she hunts up a tissue, my mind is back in the dentist's office—an episode just five hours old, when my seven-year-old son needed his mother. I cradled his head and spoke reassuringly to calm his fears as Dr. Jeff worked to fix a tooth. That sweet little boy. Sally is right. It is a different relationship—certainly different from the tender and tenacious bond between a mother and daughter.

"You know," Sally says, returning to the couch, "I've decided grieving is a very personal and lonely thing. A private thing. Lloyd was often angry at God, you know, feeling like Vaughn's death was unfair. I guess I just prefer to love a God who holds me up through all this.

"And God did. Look, we had no house to take care of and maintain. Our rent was considerably lower than a house payment. We hadn't moved to a strange town. We had great insurance coverage. We had a wonderfully supportive church and school community, and that amazing staff at Doernbecher Children's Hospital. There was Vaughn's own indomitable spirit, and I had the summer off from school to be with him.

"He died in the summer, which was much easier to handle than during the rainy season."

I look at her, amazed. Throughout Mom's struggle, I spent very little time thanking God for his mercies. Mostly I just begged for a cure. Today, six years removed from my mother's death, I am certain: thanksgiving is foundational to healing.

Sally continues. "Carol, it doesn't mean it doesn't hurt. It's just that in the midst of the agony, there are kindnesses. God acted on my behalf. God will act on yours."

I leave her home, silenced to my core. Sally has taught me all right, taught me that even in grief I have choices. I can embrace anger or embrace "a God who holds me up through all this." I can begin a season of thanksgiving and allow God's healing presence to work on my battered heart.

Grief is physically, emotionally and spiritually painful. It is lonely, because no one has lost the person I know but me. Looking at these realities squarely, I can be thankful or bitter, grateful or negative, held close or flailing away. The way I deal with loss is by making choices. One of those choices is whether or not to acknowledge the small kindnesses, the graces that accompany us through such times.

Bonnie, another woman in my Monday night class, called this week to remind me of the importance of thankfulness. In her fifties and a mother of four, Bonnie lost her husband of thirty years to heart failure three years ago. For Bonnie, John's homegoing was devastating. He was her life. She did not believe she would last a month.

This week Bonnie called to tell me she was giving a thank-you dinner. Shortly after John's death, a group of singles came and made Bonnie a part of their circle. They invited her to dinners, included her on beach trips, phoned and listened endlessly to a widow's grief.

Today Bonnie, who is a remarkably strong woman to begin with, has found her footing. She calls on other widows, being the arms of the church that hold widows in their first flush of grief. Once she found herself in a shopping mall with an elderly man whose wife had just collapsed of a heart attack. There too the comfortless became the comforter. She was able to pray as one who knows the pain.

Today she teaches a grief recovery class, a very special way to say thank you. And she is grateful. Hoping to acknowledge in some small way the gift of love and support given to her when she most needed it, she is giving a dinner to say thanks. And her thankful heart teaches us all.

HE PROMISES PRESENCE

Grief is more demanding than I could have imagined. I have tested the waters. I have been engulfed by it. But the one thing I have taken away from it is a knowledge that God is present. God will sustain me.

As my mother's life came to a close, the hospice nurse tried to help me understand that Mother would be gone very soon. I did not understand her words. Mom was still talking to me on a daily basis. She knew me. We prayed together.

That night I had a profound dream. Somehow, in this darkest season of my life, God was invading my dreams. It went like this: I was kneeling in our church sanctuary, praying diligently about some unknown need. In that sanctuary was a lovely cross with a carved figure of Christ on it. It was not the crucified Christ, but Christ the king. In my dream, Christ spoke to me from that cross and said, "It is finished, Carol." I seemed perfectly content with that and rose from my knees to sit in the pew. A woman was speaking from the pulpit. I listened to her for a few moments and then she came and stood behind me, hugging my shoulders. At that moment, I heard the Lord say, "I will be your mother."

That was the dream. The next evening, my mother went home to be with her Savior, and while I grieved as a motherless child, I was also comforted. God would be my mother. God would nurture me and care for me. I could rest under the wings of God.

God was present in a hundred separate ways during those days. He made sure Diane called the morning after mother passed. "Carol, honey, I just can't get you off my mind. What is going on?" I told her that Mom had died, and she said, "So that is why I keep hearing the Spirit whisper your name!" She comforted me, reminding me that in the life of a Christian, these days are the very best of the very worst.

Joan did not know Mom was dying, only that she was ill. Yet Joan felt compelled to write me a note, sending a Scripture that speaks of comfort. I received the note as I came home from Mom's deathbed. Another sister in Christ, Cathy, was on the phone immediately, and it has been Cathy who has marked my path in the journey of grief.

I was surrounded by love, surrounded by God's presence. I was also filled with a certainty that Mom was with Jesus. I had no doubt, no conflict about her passing. She was in the presence of the Creator. My creative little Mama, lunching with the Creator!

I miss her. Six years, ninety-nine days and fourteen hours later, I still can be doubled over with grief. I miss her laughter. I miss her advice. I miss being able to pick up the phone and tell her the latest escapades of my children. I will miss her until I see her again.

That is the strength of our hope. I am convinced that I will see Jesus face to face. And right behind him, I'll see Mom, anxiously awaiting her chance to embrace me. That is the joy of my salvation. And it is a joy that has been carefully taught, coached, encouraged and rejoiced in by my circle of mentors—my sisters.

Mary Magdalene knew that joy. Having experienced the hopelessness of death, she heard Jesus call her name. She saw him; she heard him; she touched him with eager hands. She knew better than I what it is to celebrate the joy of our salvation. It is Mary's story, thousands of years removed from mine, that anchors me to this hope. She knew the joy. Someday you and I will know it fully also. We will celebrate the resurrection within the shadow of the cross.

FOR REFLECTION AND DISCUSSION

1. Read John 14:1-4. Who do you know that has been through the grief process? What have you learned from them? What have you learned from grief in your own walk? Who needs your special touch today?

How Do We Stay United?

. . . .

The woman came and knelt before him. "Lord, help me!" she said.

He replied, "It is not right to take the children's bread and toss it to their dogs."

MATTHEW 15:25-26

THE CANAANITE WOMAN'S STORY

I don't think I'm all that different from most people. After all, you're raised a certain way, exposed to certain beliefs, and to be honest, in all my dealings with the Jews prior to him, I found nothing to change my beliefs.

All in all they are a lazy race of people. They deal with money—not with the honest labor of our Canaanite men. I employ some of their number in my household, and they require constant supervision. Lazy. Undisciplined.

I'll tell you, if it's a Jewish maid you train, you'd have an easier time with a dog. Lazy, ill-tempered. Turn your head for a moment and it's another chance for her to take a break. They simply don't know how to work. That's all. It's not prejudice; it's common knowledge.

So when my daughter became afflicted in her mind, you can guess I did not try a Jewish physician. No. Two years of doctors. One from Rome, one from Samaria, four Canaanites. No luck. I still had a mentally unbalanced child.

Do you know what it is like to have a child like that? The neighbors talk, that's what it's like. People talking. People pointing. Ugly rumors of demon possession. Well, not my daughter. It's just a fever. A small storm in her brain that will pass.

This is what I told myself during these two full years of searching for a cure. Two years of watching her disintegrate before my very eyes. So, when my faithful Canaanite housekeeper told me of a healer, I was ready. Grace had begun to cut herself and had to be watched around the clock. I was at my wits' end. Imagine. Cutting herself. So, when the housekeeper suggested the Jew, I was ready to try anything, even a Jew.

It was a hot day. The breeze of the late afternoon was not present. I felt the exhaustion of two years of battle weighing heavily upon me. I'll tell you the truth: two blocks from where the Jew was staying, I almost turned back.

A Jew. Might as well train a dog. But the doctors had not healed my daughter.

"Lord, Son of David," I cried out, "have mercy on me! My daughter is suffering terribly from demon possession." I worded it carefully— fully aware of the Jewish fetish for demons.

He turned and studied me.

I'll tell you the truth. This man was no Jew. Not like the ones I'd known. *He did not say anything.*

I'm not accustomed to dealing with silence. The last silent moment I remember was before I married. Jesus invited me to be still. To recognize something. To . . . but never mind. I just repeated my request, louder and louder. I followed them and cried openly.

Soon hot tears of frustration and humiliation steamed off my face. Here was a Jew. Refusing to speak to me. Refusing to help me. All he offered was silence.

I did not like this new position. I am used to running the show.

I don't like silence and I don't like to ask for anything, let alone beg. And now I was forced to do both and to act like a common laborer.

By now his followers were asking him to silence me. I was on their nerves. *They were treating me like I had treated so many Jews asking for work. They were treating me like I treated Jews.*

Slowly he turned and studied me once again. His eyes held the knowledge to cure my daughter and return her to us. What? I wanted to cry out. What do you want from me?

"I was sent only to the lost sheep of Israel," he said. So that was it. He knew I viewed his sheep as dogs. He knew I saw no value in them. He knew.

I knelt before him. Knelt. Amazed to find myself in a kneeling position but glad to give up the struggle. Glad to rid myself of the hatred. I could kneel before a Jew and know him as my superior. I could kneel with other Jews and know them as my equals. I could even serve them. I could change.

"Lord, help me," I begged.

"It is not right to take the children's bread and toss it to their dogs," he said, his eyes soft and smiling.

I smiled back. "Yes, Lord," I replied, "but even the dogs eat the crumbs that fall from their master's table."

He nodded. "Woman," he said, "you have great faith! Your request is granted."

Great faith. He said I had great faith. Well, that certainly puts a new face on things, doesn't it? A woman of great faith must hold on to her revelations. A woman of great faith must not discriminate against Jews or any other people. A woman of great faith. This would take a total change in living. One I determined to make.

So Grace was done with her small brain storms, and I . . . I was freed of my demons.

THE GOAL OF UNITY

I have often wondered about the Canaanite woman's story. Why would Jesus answer her in such a way? History tells us that the Jews referred to the Canaanites as dogs. I began to wonder if the woman referred to the Jews in a similar fashion. I do not know what the reality of that situation was, but I do know that Jesus chose those words for a reason. I am convinced that he did not view people as we view them, but instead saw us as part of a large family, the family of God. He viewed our differences as powerful reasons to rejoice. He passionately desired a unified family of God, rejoicing in their differences as well as their similarities. He wanted an end to the cutting remarks and putdowns.

The chapters in John that deal with Jesus' last evening with his disciples have always moved me. With the cross just hours away, he prayed that we might be unified: "I in them and you in me. May they be brought to complete unity to let the world know that you sent me and have loved them even as you have loved me" (John 17:23).

In this section of Scripture he commands that we love one another and then begs the Father for unity. It is an interesting prayer and a poignant moment as Christ prepares to leave his disciples.

Having been a part of church life for forty-some years, I know the wisdom of that prayer. Nothing is more needed than a firm commitment to loving one another. Nothing is a better witness to the world than unified sisters. Nothing.

The goal for the church is to be a unified representation of her Lord, but how in the world do we reach that goal? The problem is that often we don't know what unity looks like. We are aware of our differences but it is a rare group that has learned to live with those differences and offer grace to each other as brothers and sisters. I know of such a rare group. It is filled with women who have mentored each other as peers, as friends, as sisters.

127

Mark and I moved to our current home six years ago. We knew no one in town. Our children found our church for us because they loved the youth group. We were lonely and feeling unconnected, despite our new church acquaintances.

Into this short season of homesickness came my friend Susan. She had read my first book, and when she found out I was attending her church, she introduced herself. Susan understands hospitality of the heart better than anyone I know. She immediately asked Mark and me and the kids to their almost finished home that afternoon. By almost finished, I mean the exterior walls were up and the interior framing in place, but the sheet rock was not up. The underlayment for the floors was down, but the carpet and linoleum were not. The house was a good two months away from completion.

That afternoon she had invited a group of friends to come and write Scripture on the framing, to write blessings on the floors, to ask God's presence to be in this new home—and she asked us to join them. So Mark and I smiled at each other and went to Steve and Susan's home.

It was the beginning of a wonderful friendship. Six years later, I can't imagine life without Steve and Susan and the circle of friends they made us a part of. I have learned much of what I know about how to parent adolescents from this circle of friends.

Not only have Mark and I been blessed, but our children have as well. Steve and Susan's daughters are a few years older than ours. They taught my daughters' small groups, loving them and fussing over them and making sure their transition into high school was an easy one. Mark and Lisa's daughter and son have been incredibly kind to my children, providing much-needed rides to soccer practice. Mike and Susan's twins are contemporaries of our daughters. Each of our daughters gained confidence through the joking and teasing of Joe and Susan's sons. Don and Donna's son and daughter have taught my children the joy of following Jesus. Their children have now graduated and headed off to college, and this Christmas, two of their daughters will marry young men devoted to Jesus.

We are a warm and caring circle of friends. This does not mean that life has been easy. We have watched our children go through tough times, and we have not always seen things the same way. And you know how high emotions run when your children are involved! But we have loved each other continually and supported each other spiritually.

Two years ago Joe and Susan's son became a parent at seventeen. I cannot tell you the anguish involved in that event. Susan wanted to raise that child more than anything. The young mother wanted the baby to be adopted by a family three thousand miles away. Joe and Susan both wanted their son and the young woman to be whole, to be healed and to be loved by the family of God.

As they walked through this, the rest of us had opinions. Some of us thought Susan should be allowed to raise the child. Some of us thought the adoption was best. We even felt compelled to share these views occasionally (not necessarily the wisest thing to do). We all were pretty convinced of our own wisdom. But for the most part, we learned to quietly keep our mouths shut and find our knees. We learned to love and leave the decisions to those involved, to be supportive and trust God with the details.

So what happened? Oh, nothing much, just an incredible state of grace that ensured our unity as friends. The results of such a journey? We love each other more deeply than before. A child has a home on the East Coast, where he is loved and adored by two people who could not have children. Susan is a grandmother, and the family that adopted the baby has been generous with pictures and phone calls. Susan and Joe have visited their grandson on a couple of occasions. Their son and the young woman are both attending colleges now, each finding healing in their own ways.

Did the pain go away? I don't think so. I know Susan wants to hold that little boy every day of his life. I know their son thinks of his child constantly. But the pain has become bearable and the results seem a work of grace. Susan and Joe have taught us what it means to love your children when they do the wrong thing. Their son has taught my children about standing up and owning your mistakes. And the response of the church body has reminded all of us that we are family, forgiven by the same Lord.

Susan has mentored us in the fine art of standing strong when hopes and dreams collapse. She has shown us the tears, the sorrow and the ability to love her child and her friends. She has taught us that love is indeed the finest thing. Love is all that truly mattered. We need to learn to love.

JUDGMENT DESTROYS UNITY

Unity is something we all crave. We want circles of sisters who will love us whatever comes our way. We want sisters to trust the Holy Spirit who dwells within us. We want unity. So what gets in the way?

Judgments often destroy unity. Scripture gives us detailed instructions for dealing with conflict. In Matthew 18:15-17 Jesus outlines a specific procedure for dealing with these disagreements:

> "If your brother sins against you, go and show him his fault, just between the two of you. If he listens to you, you have won your brother over. But if he will not listen, take one or two others along, so that 'every matter may be established by the testimony of two or three witnesses.' If he refuses to listen to them, tell it to the church; and if he refuses to listen even to the church, treat him as you would a pagan or a tax collector."

Implicit in this set of instructions is knowledge that the other person has committed a sin. This means he or she has violated Scripture and you are both aware of it.

I will never forget going to Ernestine with just such a problem. I had been sinned against and I knew it. I knew the instigator knew it and I wanted help. I wanted my mentor to take care of the problem. High time she mentored someone else! I wanted the weight of her good name to force the other woman to do the right thing.

Ernestine listened to me tenderly. When I finished spilling out my wrath, she asked one simple question: "What did she say when you confronted her with this?"

Uhh . . . squirm . . . watch my shoes for a while. "I haven't exactly talked to her yet," I replied. "I thought that if you would go with me . . ."

Ernestine shook her head. "That is not what Scripture teaches. You go first, by yourself, and save face for both of you. Handle this quietly," she instructed. "I'm only available when the first step fails." What wisdom Ernestine brings to my life. First things first.

I went to the woman, shared my grievance and heard her own grievance in return. I was glad Ernestine wasn't there. I had my own repenting to do. The biblical structure saved a friendship; my over-eager approach would have destroyed it.

ONLY GOD SEES THE HEART

Another problem with judging others is that we are often wrong. Remember when Samuel wanted to anoint Saul's successor, the next king of Israel? God instructed Samuel saying, "The LORD does not look at the things man looks at. Man looks at the outward appearance, but the LORD looks at the heart" (1 Samuel 16:7). I am often guilty of looking at the outward appearance of situations and making judgments. This can be a devastating thing to do, one that can destroy unity in the body of Christ.

I have a dear friend, one who has loved me with greater kindness than I deserve. Katie is a woman who is devoted to Jesus and has been married for years. She has a kind heart and a tender way of helping young women as they learn the parenting ropes. She is regularly on the lookout for ways to show the love of Christ to others and has mentored me throughout my own parenting.

It came as a shock to me when Katie suddenly didn't want to be kind. She refused to help me throw a bridal shower. Refused. I couldn't believe it. She just said, "I can't do it. Find someone else." Now, I *knew* that she needed to throw that shower. Katie was on the women's commission. If she didn't participate, it would send a bad message. Besides, the bride was well known and loved. What could Katie possibly be thinking?

I got right back on the phone with her and told her she had to do this. She asked me to trust her and to please not make this difficult. So, I found another to help me. Katie showed up late to the shower and left early.

I found her wanting. I decided that maybe she wasn't as committed as she should be. I let a wedge enter our friendship. I judged her. Over the years we became casual friends instead of sisters. We both hurt over the loss, but I just didn't trust her. How could she have done it?

Seven years later, I found out. Seven years later, I could have died. Seven years later, I learned that Katie's husband had been involved with the bride. Very involved. Too involved. And I wanted her to throw the "other woman" a bridal shower. Sometimes you just want the earth to swallow you whole.

Did I tell you that Katie is kind? Katie forgave me and let a friendship be restored. Today she smiles at me with her mouth and with her eyes. She is my sister again. An act of grace in her heart has allowed the unity Christ prayed for to become a reality in our relationship. She has taught me, coached me, loved me back into unity. She is a mentor par excellence.

DISPUTABLE MATTERS

Sometimes conflicts arise and there are no clear-cut answers. When this happens, emotions often run high. We have our opinions that matter to us deeply, and yet there is no scriptural guideline that we can all agree on. My sisters have mentored me in this arena also. They have listened to my passion and helped me work through my response.

It happened shortly after I had been asked to serve on a church board. We had a friendly group and often held similar views. We wanted our church to be Christ in this small town. We did things other churches did not in an effort to meet the hurting. Our church had a soup kitchen, tutors for migrant workers' children and several different ministries to help those society was neglecting. I loved my work with this church board.

As part of our outreach we allowed Alcoholics Anonymous and Narcotics Anonymous to meet in our building on a weekly basis. We had funds to deal with the janitorial problems this caused. We had a pastor whose son battled an addiction, and we were committed to helping any way we could.

The problem arose when the women who cared for our building asked the board to have the AA and NA groups stop smoking on the premises. Although they were smoking outside the building, it seemed to creep indoors. The smoke was causing problems with paint and fabrics, and the secondhand smoke was a health concern.

This sounded like an easy issue to me. In the Northwest, smoking has long been out of vogue. I thought we would just agree and ask them to stop. I was wrong.

Our pastor brought in the AA leader. Together they explained that when a person is trying hard to kick one addiction, he or she sometimes needs the crutch of another addiction, nicotine. If we prohibited smoking, many would find it too difficult to endure. Our pastor asked us to increase the janitorial budget and allow them to continue to smoke outside the building, to love them in this way. He said our church was Jesus' house, and Jesus would invite them in.

We were not convinced, at least not all of us. We argued. We debated the ethics of allowing anyone to smoke on the premises. We discussed the frustration of higher janitorial bills. We questioned the premise of the AA leader. We argued among ourselves, and on this issue we couldn't reach consensus.

Finally we voted. As a group we passed an agreement to allow them to continue smoking outside the main door. It was a very close vote. We left quietly, not chattering happily on our way to our cars. It was a walk filled with sideways glances and pursed lips.

I was frustrated and thought that we should reconsider. I went to my circle of sisters, shared my distress and listened to their advice. It was a new problem for all of them. None of them attended my church, but they understood its mission and they loved the impact it was having on the lost of that town.

My sisters also understood my temperament. They knew that I was likely to share my distress and frustration with several sources as I worked it through, so they suggested silence. They suggested I take my concerns to the cross and silently ask Jesus for peace and for his mind in this matter.

Paul instructed the church not to argue about disputable matters. This was a disputable matter. It was an emotional minefield but not one the Scriptures speak to specifically. Both sides could find biblical texts to support their point of view. Yet the continuing conflict threatened to destroy the unity of the body. My lack of ease with the situation could be used by the enemy of our souls to provoke trouble.

My friends wisely encouraged silence and prayer. Wise women, my sisters. Several of us on the board followed their advice, and when several months had passed, we were able to hear an update on the process without emotion. We agreed to disagree and to keep the unity between us at all costs. Our overarching goals were to reach the lost and to love each other, and we were determined to focus on those goals.

BRIDGE BUILDING

For many of the women in my church, our goals have come to include bridge building. Go—build bridges between people, help them to love each other and help each other. Get people to stop judging their brothers and sisters and begin building bridges to each other.

Too often judgment is the norm. The homeschool mothers judge private school mothers. The private school mothers judge public school mothers. And the public school mothers judge whoever is left. Those who have children judge those who have none. Married mothers judge single mothers. Single women judge married women. Working mothers are a target for mothers who stay home.

This is so much nonsense. We were none of us elected judge. We are commanded to love and support. We are to be known for our love and our compassion and our mercy. Yet often we waste time judging and fighting among ourselves over nothing. What a difference it would make if all our churches were filled with believers who simply trusted the Holy Spirit in each other, loved one another and tended to their own inner lives.

Perhaps one of the most important lessons my sisters have taught me is that judgments are often superficial. Who would have thought that unity was more important than concerns about secondhand smoke? Or that a wounded woman was protecting her healing process, not arbitrarily refusing to throw a shower? Who am I to judge my sister? Nowhere do I see Jesus telling me to do that.

There is a story in a Susan Howatch novel in which one priest is sent to deal with another priest. The second priest has been drinking. His ministry is in shambles. He is a disgrace. Rather than judging him, the messenger says that he was sent to study the man's cross and figure out the best way to get him off it.

I like that. My job is not judgment but mercy—compassionate mercy that works to remove my friends and family from the crosses that hold them captive, crosses that frequently are destroying them. Then, if I am really lucky, they will help me with mine. That mercy, that compassion is at the core of unity. I am not to judge, but to study my loved ones' suffering and figure out how to help get them down off their cross. That compassion will bring about united people and ultimately a united church, one that is known for its love.

FOR REFLECTION AND DISCUSSION

1. How does man judge? How does God judge? Look up 1 Samuel 16:7 and Galatians 2:6 for some answers.

2. Who is to judge? Read James 4:12 and Hebrews 10:30.

3. Christ, the judge, came in a spirit of reconciliation. Read John 3:17. What was Christ's mission? Is your life's mission the same? Are there actions in your life that are out of line with a spirit of reconciliation?

4. Who do you know that is good at bridge building? Can you ask him or her to help you build bridges also?

How Do I Walk in Faith?

. . . .

When he had said this, Jesus called in a loud voice, "Lazarus, come
out!" The dead man came out, his hands and feet wrapped with
strips of linen, and a cloth around his face.

JOHN 11:43-44

MARY OF BETHANY'S STORY

A woman of faith? Me? I think you mean my sister Martha. I was
known for sitting at the feet of Jesus, but it was Martha who met him
at the gate, wanting an answer. You've read the story. You know that
Martha voiced her unswerving belief that day, naming him the Christ.
Telling him that even then it was not too late.

Too late. Those two words had become my mantra and her statement of profound faith. For me, it was too late. Too late. Jesus, you
are just too late. Too late for Lazarus and certainly far too late for me.
Only Martha held out hope. Only Martha knew it was not too late.

Your hesitation, Jesus, your lingering . . . lingering with a crowd of
adoring followers while my brother fought for air, while he heaved his
body forward in an effort to catch air. Too late, Jesus. Much too late.

The air was unreachable. My brother surged toward air that
evaded his lungs while you surged toward adoring followers. Others
needed your touch; others needed a word from you. I despised those
others. We needed you here.

I listened to Lazarus gasp for air. I listened to that death rattle. I looked for your miracle-working form and watched death's features invade my sweet brother's face. I watched a death mask settle over his fine features. I watched the glaze take the eyes, and I knew that you were too late to be my Lord. You were too late.

A piece of me had shattered and died on the deathbed with my brother. My spirit felt as dead as the waxen claws that were my brother's lifeless hands. My spirit, you see, had groped after a fleeing faith just as my brother had gasped for air.

"Mary, the master is calling."

Martha. Good old full-of-faith Martha. Waiting at the gate, full of hope, still believing. And now he wished to see me. I moved on wooden feet, out of the house and toward the Christ. I could not bring my eyes to meet his. My eyes traveled no higher than his sandals.

He stroked my hair, asking Martha to take him. Take him to the place where my brother lay rotting in the grave.

So we went. Jesus, speaking softly to me, asking questions I could not answer, encouraging conversation when I could not choke out the sobs, let alone the words. Instead I nodded, wiping my eyes, watching his feet, and finally we arrived.

My legs washed out from under me and I found myself on my knees, unable to move closer. Still not able to understand that my handsome, laughing brother lay cold within this place.

A sound to my right startled me. It began as a growl and swiftly moved to the unpracticed sobs of a great man crying. I find it difficult to hear a man weep. To know that his soul has been torn in two as clearly as my own.

His sobbing was deep and wretched. It carried with it such an intensity of sorrow that even I was willing to forgive the tardiness that cost my brother his life.

"Have them move the stone," Jesus cried harshly. Martha and I moved as one to calm our Lord. To remind him that these days in the tomb would have a natural result: the odor would be overwhelming.

"Lazarus, come forth!" Jesus commanded.

The stone, which moved while we fussed at Jesus, had a shadow. Shielding my eyes from the blinding rays of the sun, I drew a deep breath and finally looked for the source of the shadow.

My brother. My dear, beloved brother. Upright. Struggling to walk. Laughing at us, shouting at us. Alive.

It would be days before I could let him out of my sight. Days before I could have a dinner and thank my sovereign with a token bottle of nard. Days before I would recognize the pulse of my spirit and know that I too had been resurrected.

He called forth my brother and brought him from death to new life. He called forth the dead place in me and gave it being. But you see, it was Martha whose faith stood the test. Martha believed, even when Lazarus was dead.

· · · · · ·

WHAT IS FAITH?

I love the old King James rendition of Hebrews 1:1, the definition Scripture gives us of *faith:* "Now faith is the substance of things hoped for, the evidence of things not seen." The New International Version says it this way: "Now faith is being sure of what we hope for and certain of what we do not see." What an incredible quality, faith. The substance of things hoped for—sure of what we hope for and certain of what we do not see.

When Mary met the risen Lord, she was seeing and hearing the substance of things hoped for. She had walked with what love and faith she possessed, and she was rewarded with a clearer understanding of God. She saw God. It is a faith and love I envy. A faith I want to possess.

My mentors have been gracious to teach me about faith. They have taught me what it is to be confident of what we hope for, certain of what we do not see. They have shown me what it looks like and allowed me to walk around in faith's landscape. They made me comfortable with faith's contours long before I would cry out to live in its dominion.

Today my friend Wendy is facing a crisis. Her greatly loved husband John is battling kidney cancer. Two years ago, one kidney was removed. This summer, the cancer is back. Kidney cancer is rare and unpredictable. When it returns, as it has in John's case, there is nothing conventional medicine can do.

Wendy came to Jesus as a young adult, a child of the sixties. She has spent her adult life loving John and loving Jesus. Her enjoyment of organic gardening, health food and nature has also been a constant in her life. We have all learned from her love of nature.

Now John may be dying. Really dying. I mean, he looks normal, he sounds normal, but as he says, the outlook is not so good. Knowing that alternative forms of medicine are the only true hope they have, John recently went to Chicago to attend a conference that spells out all the trial studies available to those who have no hope.

Wendy and John are confident that God is with them. They are aware of his presence, certain of his love. And so, with a host of friends praying daily, John and Wendy are living moment by moment. They have numbered their days and inclined their hearts to wisdom. Wendy is memorizing her husband's face. It is a tender agony to watch.

In the midst of this, I am crying out to God. "Are you there? Are you aware? How can this happen?"

Wendy is answering my cries for me. "Of course God is here. Have I told you what has happened? Have I told you about Chicago?"

I listen and find that when all the "slice and dice" (John's phrase) talk from the doctors was concluded, when John was at the end of his faith, he attended this meeting of patients. There a man stood and told his story. He had John's cancer and has now been cancer-free for three years. He is setting up a trial in Hawaii for those with kidney cancer. It is a program of nutrition and holistic therapies. It is the program for John and Wendy.

Imagine: without hope, the Lord directs them to the one program that fits their own medicinal convictions. John is one of six patients accepted. And while we do not know if John will live another twenty or thirty years or go home to Jesus soon, we do know that God has not forgotten. God is present. And that truly is the greatest gift of all.

HOW FAITH GROWS

We all want to respond as John and Wendy have responded. We all want to be confident of God's goodness, of God's presence, of God's intervention on our behalf. How do we get to such a place in life? How do we allow our faith to grow, to let God handle the true earthquakes of the spirit?

I asked Ernestine this question fifteen years ago. Watching others battle difficulty with grace, I asked her to teach me their faith. I wanted her to teach me how to stand strong and be faithful. I wanted to walk with their faith, integrity and courage.

I'll never forget Ernestine's answer: Start small. She suggested that I begin by trusting God each time my little girls were in the care of another. She recommended that I thank God for the joy they would have, for the peace and quiet I would have, and then cease to worry. She encouraged me to be faithful in the small details of life.

I watched this play out in my friends' and mentors' lives a hundred times. I watched Deb write a check to the church as she struggled to pay her bills. I watched Lori remain faithful to a difficult eating program to bring honor to her Lord. I watched several women raise children alone, and raise them with wisdom and grace.

I think of Cathy when I think of those who are faith-full. Cathy has had lupus for seventeen years, that awful autoimmune disorder that attacks the body's cells and tissues, causing pain and exhaustion. She is also raising two sons in one military base after another. She is full of pain and full of faith.

Cathy is an instinctive "nester." She delights in having a home, loving every element of homemaking and doing a beautiful job of it. She also loves Bob. She knows that God has called her husband to be in the military. This means that for the last nineteen years, Cathy has made her home wherever Uncle Sam directs. She has lived in Ohio, Alabama, South Carolina, Virginia, California and Hong Kong and has recently been told to look forward to Buenos Aires.

Cathy and Bob have lived in government housing or rentals all of their married lives. She has antiques, pictures, keepsakes, dishes from her mother and grandmother—all in storage. But she has been careful not to put their lives in storage. She has not said, "I have this disease and when I am healed, then we will really live." Instead she has worked around the disease, asking God to show her the lessons it can teach. She has not said, "I don't like living in an apartment. After we leave this assignment, we will build a house and then I will make a home." Instead she has quietly built a home wherever Bob is posted.

Cathy reminds me of Martha. There is much in Cathy's life that she does not understand. There is much that she could grieve over, reasons why she could give up. Like Martha, Cathy just keeps returning to Jesus, whatever the circumstances. She believes that home is truly a place of the spirit, not of real estate. She knows that God is our true home. Through her efforts to build a home in all the parts of the globe where they have lived, she has taught us all about home and God, who is our eternal home.

Cathy is convinced that the illness she struggles with daily is not unknown to God. She knows that God is working through the illness to teach her many things and to teach others as well. She is confident of what she cannot see. Full of faith. I have been blessed to have such mentors in the arena of faith.

Strengthened by Another's Faith

My mother's faith provided strength for me as we walked through her final illness. Turning each area of our lives over to Jesus removes the fear, the distraction and the anxiety.

Mom was diagnosed with a rare form of cancer in 1994. It was a shock to all of us. The doctor told my father and sister that she could be gone in days or last a few months. No one told my mother her time was so short. She knew the disease was terminal. She did not have knowledge of her doctor's timeline.

Mom chose to make those final years teaching time. She taught us as deeply and profoundly as possible. She taught by example, reminding us daily that all our days were written in his book before there was one of them. She rested, as much as she was able, in his sovereignty. She did not let me see fear, only confidence.

I remember her telling me that the cancer was a gift. Spiritually she had grown more in those short months than she could have believed possible. I winced at her words. I was not finding any gift in this situation. I was hurting. I recall her taking my hand and reminding me of the truth of Psalm 90:12: "Teach us to number our days aright, that we may gain a heart of wisdom." Mom was discovering what truly mattered, and she did not want her girls to miss the lesson. She wanted us to concentrate on things of eternal value.

It was two years before the cancer gained the upper hand. When it did, Mom had about a month of pain. This was difficult for all of us. And in this season also, Mom had a lesson for us. She placed a quote on the refrigerator, where all of us were bound to read it several times a day: "A season of suffering is a small price to pay for a clearer view of God" (Max Lucado).

Mom was on a journey I could not understand and often resented. I wanted her to stay with me. I wanted her to live until I was too senile to know she was gone. God had other plans. Mom wanted to teach me about the comfort of his plans. Mom trusted her Lord and looked forward to meeting him. Mom didn't want her daughters' love for that same Lord endangered.

The last spring Mom was alive, her backyard was like a Monet watercolor. Her irises were incredible. The rhododendrons were superb—the colors took your breath away. It was in this setting that I asked Mom if she was afraid. I will never forget her response. She smiled with the enjoyment of a confident child and said, "Honey, sometimes when I am out here, when I see God's glory in my own backyard, I think about where I am going. This is the fallen garden. Imagine what heaven will be like. Sometimes I am so filled with joy I want to lift my hands to the sky. It is only when I see you, or your dad or sister, that the joy leaves me."

That faith, that clear, visible faith strengthened my own.

Three months later she was enjoying heaven's landscape. Today I look out over my own garden. It is such a pretty picture. It speaks Jesus to me over and over again. It also speaks Mom. It reminds me that this is just a fallen garden. And I lift my head to heaven, comforted, and ask, "Mom? What is it like there?"

REASSURED BY FAITH

In August 2001 I was faced with my own faith walk. The semester had just begun and I was back in class when a call came from my doctor. I was to come to her office immediately. When I arrived there on a late afternoon, she informed me that there was a large growth on my ovary.

There were three possibilities. I might have endometriosis, but endometriosis is normally incredibly painful and I had experienced no pain. I might have a malignancy that was contained and could be removed without further treatment. The third possibility was what had her pale. The symptoms were all there for ovarian cancer.

I can remember little of the rest of that appointment. I know I repeatedly told her, "I have three babies to raise. I have three teenagers." She tried to reassure me. She said that if it was ovarian cancer, I would probably still have a couple of years.

Surgery was scheduled for forty hours later. Those were the longest, most terrifying, most educational forty hours of my life. In those forty hours, I learned that God's presence is the most valuable gift a person can have. And God is with us. God comforts us. God's family prayed for us—often waking at two in the morning, when I also woke in fear. They prayed through the night as God comforted Mark and me, and we fell asleep again. They prayed as we slept.

My family in faith also cared for my three children. No one was left alone. No one was uncared for. The night prior to surgery, I began to feel that God was going to allow me to live. It was just a scary sense that this would not be cancer. It was scary because it was too good to be believed. I was afraid to hope, afraid to believe.

That night four couples came to lay hands on us and pray for us. As they walked into my home, Joe said, "Relax, it won't be cancer! I've been praying!" He fairly shouted the words, and while I was afraid to believe it, it matched what God's Spirit was whispering to my soul. Joe believed when I could not. Joe had faith for both of us.

The next day, Wendy came and met us at the hospital. She prayed peace into my crazed emotions. She literally took me into her arms and prayed peace. Penny and Karen came and prayed. A small congregation of believers met Mark and Dad in the waiting room and prayed as they waited.

God was gracious to me, to my little family. It was endometriosis, the size of a cantaloupe! It would mean a complete hysterectomy, but I would recover nicely. As one doctor told me, "Now you can live into your eighties!"

I cannot begin to tell you the gratitude I felt. I kept asking nurses, "How can I begin to repay the goodness of God?"

It was a faith walk for all of us. Even in the midst of our greatest fears we believed that God was with us. We did not know if God would heal me on this earth, but we knew that ultimately he would heal me. We knew, beyond any doubt, that if he called me to his house, Mark and I would see each other again. We knew it in our bones. We knew what we could not see, what we had no rationale for.

CONFIDENT OF WHAT WE DO NOT SEE

I have always been stubborn. For me, faith has come to mean a spiritual form of confidence that is uncanny in its perception and stubborn in its belief. I like the idea of stubbornness being redeemed and put into a spiritual context where it becomes a strength.

Like Wendy, I believe in the goodness of God. I will give thanks. I will celebrate his hand in my life and in theirs, even when I do not like the circumstances he is working through. Like so many of my sisters, I am striving to be faithful in the small details of daily living. I am learning to trust the Holy Spirit in the lives of my children.

And those times when my world falls apart, I will again be mentored by the Holy Spirit to trust in God's goodness. I will be schooled by the family of God to trust in his love. I will be held safe by their love and by his until the day he takes me home. Home to Jesus' house.

FOR REFLECTION AND DISCUSSION

1. Read Hebrews 11. In your own words, write a definition of *faith*.

2. In Hebrews 11, we have the Faith-Full Hall of Fame. Whose story

do you particularly enjoy? Why?

3. If you were to nominate a mentor or friend for the Faith-Full Hall of Fame, who would it be and why?

4. What area in your own life needs the gift of faith? Who could mentor you in this area?

How Can I Hope?

· ·

*But Joshua spared Rahab the prostitute, with her family and all
who belonged to her, because she hid the men Joshua had sent as
spies to Jericho—and she lives among the Israelites to this day.*

JOSHUA 6:25

RAHAB'S STORY

Sometimes life just does not work out as planned. I know, prostitution is more than a slight bend in the road. As a religious woman once told me, "You don't want to be a whore? Stop dressing like one!" As if it were that easy.

No, life was just not what I had planned. And then the rumors began. We heard about Joshua and the Israelites. We knew that their God was the God of heaven and the God of earth. We were terrified of them because they would surely be our end.

Prostitution does many things to a woman. It certainly hardened my heart. It also taught me to look out for myself and to make deals to whatever advantage I could. I never was the hooker with a heart of gold. I was the harlot with an eye toward the main chance.

My experience with Israel was no different. I wanted to get safe passage out for my family. I wanted to live, and the two strangers who landed on my doorstep seemed the most likely way out. I needed them to like me, and sex was not on the agenda with these two.

It was while they were being served food and drink that the king sent word that he wanted the spies. I looked at the king's officers, saw their sneering acknowledgment of my profession and chose to lie. And it is not like I'm a novice to the sport of lying. I can twist truth with the best of them. "They were here," I admitted, eyes widening in feigned worry. "They left because it was getting dark and the city gate was being shut. If you hurry, you may still catch them."

They left, stupid fools. They went running after phantom spies while the real ones lay hidden on my roof. Idiots.

There was still a deal to be made. I approached the two men, explained how I would lower them to safety and made my plea. "Let me live. Let my household live. I know your God. I know his power. Let us live just as I have let you live." I did not flirt. I did not lie. I simply pleaded with these two honest men and hoped their own sense of justice would be my salvation.

I am a good judge of character. They agreed, instructing me to gather my loved ones into my home, tie a red rope out the window and wait for our saviors.

It is one thing to say it, another to live it. It was weeks before they returned. Weeks spent in a city on the verge of total collapse. Panicked people, panicked leaders, all wanting to escape the judgment of the God of Israel. I was no less terrified than my neighbors. I was busy gathering my family, busy comforting my clients, busy trying to breathe and calm my pounding heart.

The day finally arrived. The Israelites marched around the city. Then they repeated it the second day. On the third day my nerves were as raw as my neighbors'. On the fourth and fifth and sixth days I locked our doors. I could not face my neighbors. I could not look on the living dead. On the seventh day the trumpets blew and the people of Israel shouted and the walls of the city collapsed. The Israelites rushed the city, sparing only my small house, my small family.

I began to learn to hope. I began to learn that God—the God of heaven and earth—could look past my life and hope for me.

CONFIDENT EXPECTATION OF GOOD

Scripture teaches us that hope is the confident expectation of good. My friend Lexie has shown me what that looks like. She has taught me how to be hopeful of God's work in my own life, confident of God's work in the lives of my children.

Lexie's husband divorced her when her daughter was in her early teens. He had fallen in love with someone else. He needed his freedom. So off he went to "find himself" in the arms of someone else. He left devastation behind him but seemed uncaring or unaware.

Lexie's daughter Cara dealt with all the anger and unrest associated with a broken home. She was angry with both parents and wanted her family back. When her mom could not accomplish this for her, she left Lexie to live with her father and his new bride.

Three thousand miles from her daughter, Lexie grieved. Cara was now part of a home with different moral values. Cara's father had ceased to hold firm on sexual fidelity himself and now believed that if Cara wanted to experiment she needed only to be "protected."

Lexie was beside herself. "It is unlike any pain you know of. It can tear you in five different directions and it feels like it will never end," she says, her eyes tearing up even ten years later.

But Lexie endured the pain and took to her knees. She knew that Cara needed an adult encounter with Jesus. During this time, God gave Lexie promises about Cara, promises found in Scripture. As Lexie's friends took to their knees, God confirmed those promises by having friends give her the same Scriptures. Lexie began to grow strong in her conviction that God was in control. God loved Cara, and God would bring her back.

There followed a period of three years that Cara spent mostly with her father. She lived with Dad because he had looser rules than Mom. Cara wrote notes asking her mom not to contact her, to stay away.

Finally Cara's sixteenth birthday approached. Lexie was devastated that her daughter remained outside her reach. Cara had not communicated with her in months. Lexie had sent letters and cards. No response. Now a milestone in the girl's life was about to happen without her mother.

Lexie polled her friends and mentors. She asked what would be a significant gift for a sixteen-year-old girl. What would allow Cara to know that her mother was there, still loving her, still wanting to hear from her? The consensus was a pair of diamond earrings.

Lexie is a single woman without many financial resources. She works hard for her money but, as all single parents know, one income is very different from two. She saved and bought the earrings she could afford and sent them off.

It broke the ice. Cara began to call. She began to say things like, "Sure would like to see you." Lexie planned her moment and showed up unannounced. Mother and daughter were reunited.

That is not the end of the story. It really is only the beginning. Cara came home for her senior year of high school. At camp that summer, she met Jesus. The spring of her senior year, she encountered Jesus again in a powerful way, and her heart became his.

Today Cara has been on mission trips; she belongs to a church; she has a love relationship with her Savior, with her mother and with her father. It is easy to look at Cara today and forget the three years of hell her mother endured. It is easy to forget the fire that hope is forged in.

The pain for Lexie is still real. Knowing Cara's story, I am not surprised to see that, even today, revisiting those years still brings Lexie to tears. The pain was that severe. I asked Lexie how she did it. How did she stay faithful and full of hope in the face of all that? Her voice cracked as she revisited that spiritual Waterloo: "You remember what God has done in the past. You grab those promises and you hang on for all you are worth."

Confident expectation of good—Lexie has lived it. She is my mentor in hope. She shows me Jesus.

CELEBRATING HOPE

Women celebrating hope. Scripture is full of them. From Miriam dancing with her tambourine to the women at Pentecost, we are given glorious pictures of women celebrating life in Christ. We are the queens of celebration. We know how to throw a party. We bring life to the family of God through celebrations.

Last summer my family learned a lesson in celebrating hope. We had spent a few days full of heat and lines and fun at Disney World. Mark and I were tired, so we headed to the hot tub that night. It was there our lesson waited.

The Church of Holiness was sharing our hotel and the hot tub that evening. As we relaxed to the bubbles, a little grandma clad in shorts and a T-shirt proceeded to dip her first foot into the water. "Oooh, sweet Jesus, that feels good, Lord!" she cried out, opening all of our weary eyes with her joy. I smiled, knowing that I had had similar thoughts that I would never have expressed out loud. She continued down the steps, grinning and vocally praising God for the warmth of the hot tub and the relaxation it brought.

Before long, we all knew her story. Fifty-two years old, grandmother of seven, today had been her first day at Disney. Mark smiled and asked her what she had enjoyed the most. "Oh sweetness," she replied, "just being there was the best. Just being there." We smiled agreement and the conversation began to focus on the joys of the day, away from the heat and the lines and the prices of junk food.

It wasn't long before our friend had some words for us. She

turned, addressed Mark and me, and said, "Kids, you know I came expecting me a blessing!" Heads nodded around the tub. "Do you understand about expecting a blessing?" she asked. Then she reminded us, "Those who come expecting a blessing get much more than the rest."

Mark and I were profoundly moved by this grandmother. Fifty-two years old and her first day at Disney. She came expecting a blessing. She had a confident expectation of good. She knew hope.

Mark and I returned to our hotel room, where I told the children of our meeting. They loved her story and took her teaching to heart. The rest of the trip was full of reminders that sounded like this: "Mom, are you expecting a blessing today?"

Our little grandma was right. Those who come expecting a blessing get far more than the rest.

Today is the first Sunday in June. In our small congregation, ten seniors have just graduated from high school. Graduation is a time that celebrates hope. Our week began with parties for several of the girls. By Friday night, those of us without graduating seniors were sneaking out of the ceremony early to run and decorate for the graduation-night party. Twenty or thirty members of our small church were taping up streamers, positioning paper palm trees and figuring out the espresso bar. Today, sun shining and kids edgy with dreams of summer just days away, we all drove down to one family's home to celebrate the young men who were graduating. Six young men, six families, all kinds of fun in the sunshine as we as a community celebrated their success and sent them on their way with prayers of dedication.

It was a lovely end to their years at Sherwood High School. The celebration was fun for the kids and, I believe, necessary for the adults. It was important to celebrate together, to laugh and sing each student's praises. They will all be going on adventures of their own.

The time for celebrations was today. The time for preparation and goodbyes is just around the corner.

Graduation is like so many of the good times in life. We are celebrating hope. Celebrating God's work already done and looking to his work in the near future. We are often celebrating through damp eyes. Our faith in God, in his ability to bring good into their future, is solid. Our hope is defined, delineated with dreams that each mother and father has held for those children since conception. Our love for them is uncompromised by surviving adolescence with them. We have watched their pranks and difficulties and are pleased to find ourselves still deeply in love with these kids.

I have observed these mothers, knowing that my own children begin that leaving-the-nest process in just a year. I have watched these moms cry with each other. I have watched them encourage their children, assuring them that college will be wonderful. I have watched them throw parties when they wanted to sit down and sob about the end of an era in their lives. I have been mentored by the best.

Women often organize the celebrations of hope, the celebrations of life. We seem to be at the center of such events. We bring the magic to the party—as well as twenty pounds of potato salad, three cases of Dr. Pepper and endless tamales. We organize the life of the community, and celebration needs to be at the center of that life. Being a part of celebrations has taught me the power of hope—the power of mentoring children through childhood and then looking to the future with a confident expectation of God's goodness in their lives.

HOPE IS A VERB

There are many times when we don't feel like celebrating.

I think of our young friend Shawna and her sweet husband, Ben. Last summer, they buried their firstborn. Anna was stillborn. No child was more wanted, no baby more loved, and yet God allowed that little girl to visit us for only moments.

Shawna and Ben determined, in those first moments of grief-stricken shock, to trust God. Shawna carries a photo of Anna. Our church family has been privileged to grieve with this young couple, to celebrate Anna's life and her parents' love. Yes, celebrate. That little girl was deeply loved, is deeply loved, and that life deserves celebrating.

We have also prayed. Shawna and Ben want more children. Not replacements, just brothers and sisters who will know that Anna came first. For nearly a year, the dream of other children has been denied. It has not changed them. Their hope has been a clear testimony to the high school kids they work with. Their living hope has mentored all of us.

So it will come as no surprise to you that yesterday, reading my e-mail, I screamed out loud. My daughters, racing to see what had happened, read the same e-mail and whooped and hollered. Ben and Shawna are pregnant. And we celebrated by yelling and laughing.

You can bet that this is only the beginning. Women are already planning the celebrations ahead. Everywhere we go, the church body is sharing the great news. One or two dads have even been seen brushing their eyes. We will celebrate the joy of this child every day of its life. And women will be at the heart of those celebrations, planning baby showers, praying through Shawna's pregnancy and labor, bringing meals when the baby arrives. Hopeful. Full of confident expectations of God's good work in their lives. We are expecting a blessing.

Women get to lead the parade. This is how it has always been. This is how it will always be. We are the relationship builders, and celebrations build relationships. We are given the wonderful job of strengthening the community through the bonds of celebration. We plan the weddings, the graduations, the birthday parties and the anniversaries. We are there when grief takes over and we remind each other that we are still going to celebrate the life we were privileged to share, even when we are committing a body to the ground and a soul to the Father. We celebrate hope. We teach hope. We live out hope.

FOR REFLECTION AND DISCUSSION

1. Who do you know that lives a hope-filled life? How has hope inspired you in your own journey?

2. Let's look at hope's geographic location. Where does hope come from? Where does it reside? What do we hope in? Read the following Scripture passages and note your thoughts.

   - Psalm 42:5
   - Psalm 62:5
   - Psalm 119:74

3. What do we put our hope in? Are there promises attached to hope? Read the following Scripture passages and note your thoughts.

   - Psalm 130:5
   - Isaiah 40:31
   - Jeremiah 29:11
   - Romans 12:12

Conclusion

. . . .

These three remain: faith, hope and love.
But the greatest of these is love.

1 CORINTHIANS 13:13

S*ister.* My thesaurus has no synonym for it. It is unique. The relationship between sisters is one of a kind. It is a relationship we crave, one we want more than chocolate.

It is also incredibly difficult to obtain, to nurture, to protect. In Oscar Wilde's *The Importance of Being Earnest* two men are discussing the eventual meeting of two young women. One man is guardian to one woman and lover to the other. Anticipating their meeting he states, rather naively, "They will throw their arms around each other and call each other sister." His friend grimaces and says, "Women only call each other sister after they have called each other many other things first!"

We know well the reality of that statement. In this fallen world, we have been trained to call each other many things, and sister is seldom one of them. Why is that? Why have we learned every other possibility instead of the one our soul craves?

LOVING FRIENDSHIPS THAT LAST A LIFETIME

We are desperate for the love of other women. We are desperate for female voices, for that bond of sisterhood. We want friendships that last a lifetime. We want long-term love relationships within the body of Christ that begin here and continue into eternity.

In high school my mother formed a friendship with Mary Etta. They double-dated with Bill and Marv. They married Bill and Marv before their twenty-first birthdays. They were friends for life. Into that circle came John and Ginger, Cal and Virginia, Ken and Annis, Gene and Evelyn. The women formed a tight circle of sisters. They were sisters of the soul. They loved each other, loved each other's children and joked with each other's husbands.

Over the years, these women celebrated and grieved together. They had disagreements. They got hurt. But their friendship held true. They really loved each other. They mentored each other. They taught their children what it means to love for a lifetime. They became so close they began to sound like each other. Today I sometimes visit with Mary Etta, just to hear my mother's voice reflected in her speech patterns, to see Mom's love of beauty reflected in Mary Etta's home.

When Mom died, not everyone could be at the graveside. We wanted family only. These women were family. Mom was buried in a spot with a wonderful view of the valley. We said goodbye to her earthly body with my kids singing Psalm 23 in rap. Mom must have loved that.

Last winter Ginger followed Mom into that other country. As she had instructed, she was buried next to Mom. Sisters.

I visit those two graves occasionally. I know Mom and Ginger aren't there. I know where they are. I know in whose presence they laugh and tease and smile. Sometimes I just need the reminder that sisters are forever. Those women I laugh with and pray with, those women I learn from and celebrate life with are the sisters of my soul. Someday they will meet me in that other country, where we will join our mothers and worship our Savior forever. Sisters for the whole journey.

TOGETHER IN THE STRUGGLES

The whole journey. That means in the good times and in the bad times. It means when I am blessed and when I feel the alienation of a hurting soul. It means that I am committed to those sisters of mine when I want to run and hide.

Susan taught me that lesson. Just three months ago she faced a crisis involving her close circle of friends in San Jose. These women raised their children together and their spiritual bonds are tight. Susan is a part of their lives, even living eight hundred miles away.

Susan received a call: "We have breast cancer." Her friend did not say, "Diane has breast cancer"; she said "*We* have breast cancer." If one suffers, they all suffer. The circle is putting their lives on hold to respond to breast cancer.

This has been a difficult week for my family of sisters too. John and Wendy are in Hawaii battling kidney cancer. Cathy was diagnosed Monday with an aggressive form of breast cancer, and she is in Hong Kong—fifteen hours by plane. I cannot get my arms around her fast enough. "*We* have breast cancer," and I cannot be there physically to comfort her and help.

But Cathy is not alone. She tells me that Jesus is with her in powerful ways. Her circle of friends and family is rapidly checking schedules, finding stateside oncologists to recommend and adjusting plans in case she stays in Hong Kong and we need to travel to be with her.

Love always responds in ways that prioritize. It sets aside personal priorities to respond. Love is a sixteen-year-old offering her bedroom "if we can get Aunt Cathy to come here." Love is a community of believers who understand that if one member has breast cancer, *we* have breast cancer.

This is the love of sisters. This is the community we crave.

THE CHARGE

The Talmud says that every person must acquire two things in this world: a teacher and a friend. When we find a mentor, when we agree to mentor another, we have found just that—a teacher and a friend. Mentoring relationships are not one-way streets. Mentors teach and learn. They love and are loved. They listen and are listened to. It is a wonderful dance, a rich, eternal relationship.

I do not know where you are in life, but I do know that your heart is probably like mine. You want the kind of friends who school you, who love you, who are there to share the joys and be steadfast in the crises of life. This is what Titus 2 tells us to find. We need to find teachers who show us what it means to be like Jesus. We need to open ourselves to others who see Jesus in us.

You've met my circle. You've heard our stories and laughed with us. You may have even cried with us. My prayer is that you have been encouraged by Jesus' work in our lives. Our job is done here. Yours may be just beginning. Now is the time to build those relationships that you will celebrate together on heaven's shores. Who is your mentor? Who is your friend? Who do you view as a younger sister? How can you show love and care to her? How can you show your appreciation for the friends who have seen you safely this far?

Do you remember the beginning of our journey together? I did not like the word *mentor*. This certainly changed. Now, when I hear *mentor*, I see Ernestine's face as she coaches me. I hear Wendy's voice calming me. I see Penny and Susan laughing with me. I hear Debra praying for me. I see Cathy reassuring me that all will be well.

The thesaurus needs to amend its list of synonyms for *mentor*. I think *mentor* means sister. It certainly means friend.